This is a Carlton Book

First published in 1998 by Carlton Books Limited,
20 St Anne's Court, Wardour Street, London W1V 3AW

10 9 8 7 6 5 4 3 2 1

A CIP catalogue record for this book is available
from the British Library

ISBN 1 85868 497 8

PROJECT EDITOR: Roland Hall
PROJECT ART DIRECTION: Zoë Maggs
PRODUCTION: Garry Lewis
DESIGN: Sue Michniewicz
SPECIAL PHOTOGRAPHY: Matthew Ward

AUTHOR'S ACKNOWLEDGEMENTS
I would like to thank Alastair Walker, Nick Culton
and my father, Alan Berry

Printed and bound in the United Arab Emirates

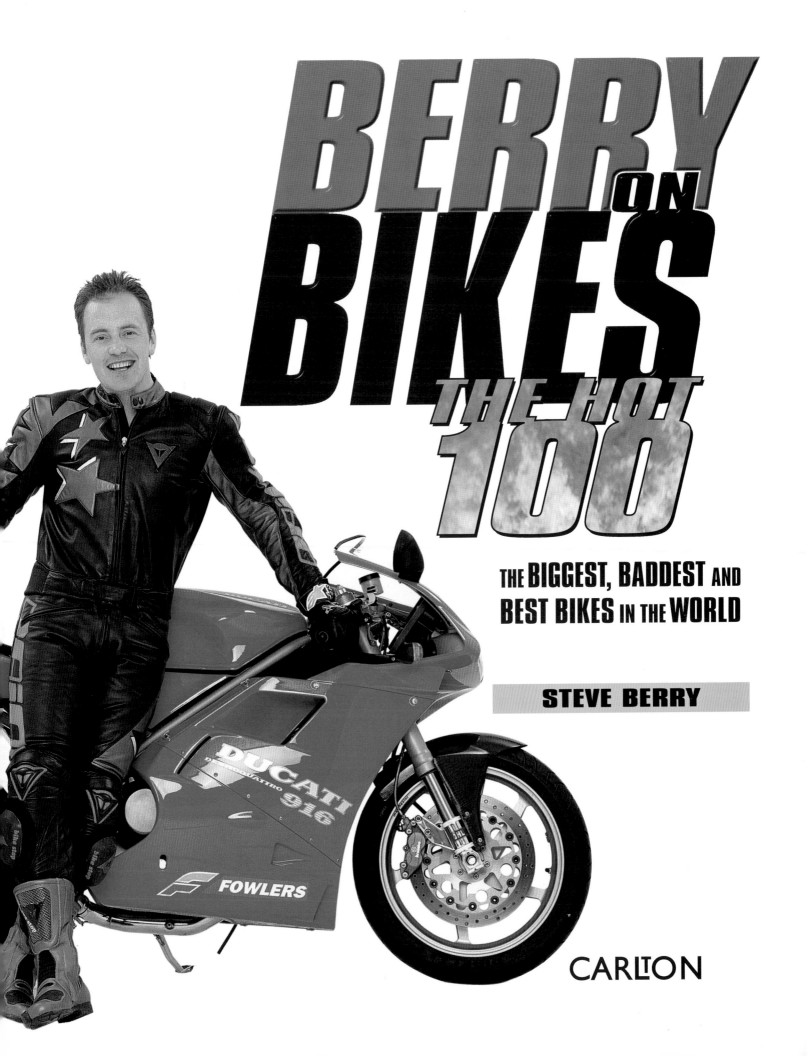

BERRY ON BIKES
THE HOT 100

THE BIGGEST, BADDEST AND BEST BIKES IN THE WORLD

STEVE BERRY

CARLTON

THE COUNTDOWN

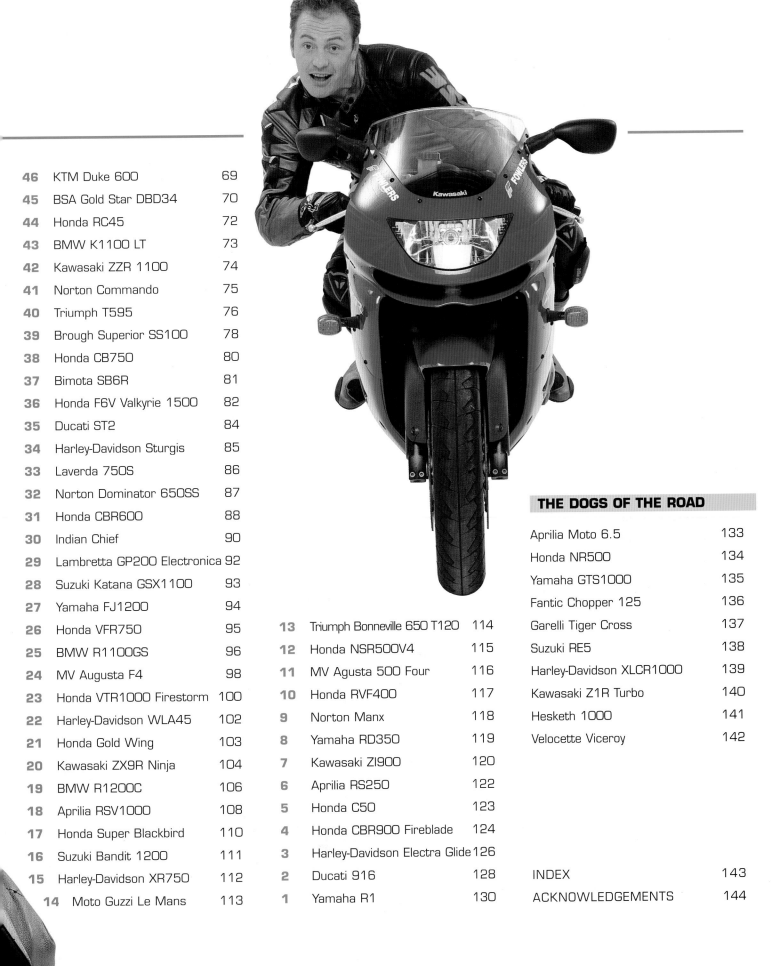

THE DOGS OF THE ROAD

INTRODUCTION

The scene is the internationally-reknowned outdoor market in Bury, Lancashire. My mother, a brunette version of Doris Day, is pushing me in my two-tone Silver Cross perambulator with its smart chrome-spooled wheels and the natty mohair convertible hood in the down position when I hear the barely-muted roar of a big British single and start waving my rattle in its general direction and squealing. Mum and dad had got together in a Heartbeat style scenario where he would affect a surley slouch outside Bury Palais trying to look like cool (tough in a PVC jacket from the Army & Navy store!) on his Ariel 1000cc replete with the de rigeur rocker rig: single-seat unit, highly-polished tank and thumb-breaking clip-on handlebars. Mum thought he looked like Tyrone Power and dad thought, well, let's not go into that.

1977. Bury Railwaymen's Club bowling green was not one of the circuits visited by the big-bucks works teams, which was just fine by us lot looking at our ramshackle collection of tired and ancient mutant machinery. The course was laid out in the classic American fashion – an

oval – although I don't think they have red cones 'borrowed' from Bury Council at Daytona or Sturgis. The only safety precautions we ever took were making sure the laces on our Doc Martens were tied. A Vespa 200cc was snatched from the steely embrace of the scrapyard crusher but needed a front tyre. Under pressure my father admitted he might have one; 'Not for highway use. Do not exceed 12mph' it said on the sidewall… it was off a wheelbarrow. Didn't stop me fitting it though. How the boys laughed an hour later as my dad drove me to casualty. 1997. The incident with the wheelbarrow tyre didn't put me off and I went on to be the editor of *Scootering*, the world's only full-colour monthly magazine dedicated to, well, the title was a bit of a giveaway. One morning the publisher says, "I've sold Scootering – how d'ya like Harleys?" Well, as it turned out, I liked them rather a lot in a strange way. But they are strange bikes. I spent the next five years working on magazines as ideologically and chronologically different as possible and sometimes in the same day I would test a Tomos in the morning for *Which Bike?* and burn rubber with the bad boys on their turbo-charged, nitrous-oxide injected projectiles on *Streetfighter*. And if I found out one thing (apart from that the cost of crashing a Bimota makes you wish you'd taken up an inexpensive hobby like polo or intercontinental powerboat racing) it was that I enjoyed almost all of it.

From the 22cc strap-on engine that is bolted to a boneshaker that hits 55mph to the Boss Hoss – a quite unfeasibly large motorcycle fitted with a six litre, 275hp Chevrolet engine and a car back tyre. But I enjoyed it, honest. So when this publisher bloke says "fancy writing a book about the fifty best bikes of all time?" I said "yeah, but let's make it the hot hundred and I'll throw in ten howling dogs for free." "Done" he says.

1998; Today, my lad Edward, aged two, pointed at my Honda Firestorm and Yamaha trials iron and said "naughty bikes". I was going to put him right, but you know, I don't think I will…

Steve Berry, Bury, July 1998

100 V8 RACER

Best banned race bike

■ Moto Guzzi Style: Carcano's shark-like masterpiece in all its glory

What's the best noise in biking? The flat drone of a big British single flying over the Mountain course? The banshee screams of a works 125cc screaming through the gears, the laid back beat of a Milwaukee-made big twin running straight-through shotgun pipes? Well, I suppose it's down to personal taste. I myself am perhaps perversely fond of the utterly antisocial racket created by a Suzuki X7 on baffle-free Allspeeds. But the strangest and most distinctive sound I ever heard coming out of a motorcycle was the one emanating from the guts of this rare and scary beast, the Moto Guzzi V8 racer.

157mph. That is the truly frightening top speed recorded by the racer in testing back in the mid-50s. Imagine doing that speed back in the 1950s on bakelite tyres with bicycle brakes to stop you.

Is it any wonder then that the FIM banned the dolphin faired V8 monster

from the rough and ready racetracks that men like Duke, Surtees and Ubbiali battled for supremecy on?

The Guzzi V8 represents the passionate, almost insane Italian spirit of speed – at all costs – within motorcycling, especially motorcycle racing. Because it struck fear and desire into the hearts of the very best racers, it's a true one-off.

Jaws on wheels.

> ‘Jaws on wheels
> … the best noise
> in motorcycling’

VITAL STATISTICS

Engine: 500cc air-cooled.
Estimated peak power: 70bhp @ 8,500rpm.
Estimated top speed: 157mph.
In 1994 Italian manufacturer Morbidelli unveiled a V8 roadbike. It was fantastically ugly and had a £90,000 price tag. No one bought one so they got top car stylist Pininfarina to give it facelift. It's still pig ugly and they still haven't sold one.

Smooth mover 70s big bike ∎

The Kawasaki Z1 900 was the undisputed King of the Superbikes back in the 70s – the Mike Tyson of its time – but just like Iron Mike, it had a few, shall we say, rough edges to it. In short, it was about as sophisticated as attending an Olympic shooting contest with a .357 Magnum and a pair of Dirty Harry sunglasses.

The Suzuki GS1000, however, was a Z1 with a Beretta in its back pocket. Slightly more subtle, but just as devastating in the right hands. The motor was an almost direct copy of Kawasaki's mighty mothership, just bigger and a tad quieter. It pumped out around 90bhp at 8,500rpm and weighed in pretty close to the Kawasaki too, but it was the refined chassis behaviour which set the Suzuki apart.

Where the Z1 would be floundering through bumpy corners, doing a rather fetching impersonation of a sumo wrestler rolling about in a vat of wet fish, the Suzuki had real aplomb. In a nutshell, it pretty much went where you pointed it, unless you decided to cash in your life insurance and go production racing on it. In fact, some people did and they even won a few races on the GS1000.

The big Suzy also had a double disc braking set-up at the front which was marginally better than most 70s dinosaurs, a comfortable dual seat, grab rail, and air-assisted suspension, giving you a smoother ride than a Saturday night in with the Bee Gees and their favourite beard strimmer.

Like so many other Japanese motorcycles, it was a well-thought-out,

VITAL STATISTICS

Engine: 997cc DOHC, four cylinder, four stroke. Gears: Five speed. Primary drive: straight cut gears. Carbs: four 34mm Mikuni constant vacuum type.
Estimated peak power: 90bhp @ 8,500rpm.
Estimated top speed: 125mph.

The white and blue GS1000S model was known in the trade as the "ice cream van."

integrated package, but remember this was back in 1978 – people were still queuing up and paying good money to buy Triumph 750 Bonnevilles, for God's sake.

The GS1000 evolved in the space of two years into possibly the most adroit, accomplished big bike of the era, the standard which everyone else – particularly Honda – struggled to beat. It was available in a shaft-driven option for touring, or a sporty nose-faired version with bigger carbs for the full-on nutcase. Paul Dunstall even managed to make one do 153mph with a full fairing on it, a proud boast which was imprinted on the side-panels of the subsequent Dunstall GS1000 replica.

For 1980, that was going some...

a smoother ride than a Saturday night in with the Bee Gees

∎ **Suzi Quattro: In the USA, they coined the term 'universal Japanese motorcycle' after the GS1000**

Weirdest Italian bike ever

There are some things in life which are simply too strange to contemplate – a quiet night in with Ken Livingstone, drinking anything from a fat woman's shoe, and staring for too long at a photograph of Enya all spring to mind. But riding a hub centre steering motorcycle is perilously close to the dark side of weird city.

Yes, there are sound engineering arguments for separating the front braking action from the steering of a racing motorcycle. But hey, Elf tried it in the 80s and it didn't win, even though Ron Haslam nearly touched his shoulders down on the corners to try and achieve that result. So it's kinda difficult to imagine there being a real benefit on roadbikes, although I'm sure that one day someone – probably BMW – will prove us all wrong-thinking Luddites.

The Bimota Tesi was one brave attempt, however, and almost beautiful to boot. Like so many great motorcycle design ideas, it owes its origin to aircraft construction.

In the 1970s a duo of free thinkers called Mead and Tomkinson built a Kawasaki engined, hub centre steered machine called "Nessie" in the UK, which had an alloy spaceframe wrapped around the engine – similar to the way in which an aircraft engine is mounted to cope with massive metal-bending stresses. The fuel tank was slung under the engine, to help weight distrubution.

Trick stuff, but it all came to nothing, like so many other great British worldbeaters of the

70s, such as Aztec bars, Derby County and Legs & Co.

However, an Italian engineering student called Pierluigi Marconi must've been paying attention at the back, because in

1983 he got himself a job at Bimota by publishing his university thesis – in Italian, thesis is *tesi* – on alternatives to

■ **It's mad, but strangely normal to ride**

> *'riding a hub centre steering motorcycle is perilously close to the dark side of weird city'*

to telescopic forks on motorcycles.

Bimota built a prototype and took it to Milan for the autumn bike show to blow a few minds wide open. Which it did.

Like Nessie, the Tesi featured a spaceframe wrapped around an engine, except this one was made by Swiss conglomerate Ciba-Geigy out of a sort of honeycombed hardboard – kind of a NASA meets MFI deal. Later Tesi models however got a stunning frame in cast alloy, cast in an inverted, twin spar arrangement – it looked like a small bridge arched across from the front of the engine to the back.

Pretty radical, but there was more. The bike had a conventional swinging arm at the back, but up front there was a hub centre arrangement, using what looked like a swinging arm fork set forwards from the engine.

Steering, as in actually turning the front wheel sideways, was achieved using hydraulically operated arms set parallel to the two arms which held the front wheel. Is your brain hurting yet?

Being Italian, the Tesi was fitted with utterly divine bodywork, enormously sexy exhausts and a digital instrumentation panel which either brings to mind *Blake's 7* or the dashboard of an Austin 1300 Traveller, depending on your age.

The surprise comes when you detach all that beautifully fastened plastic and discover a rather basic Ducati V-twin engine underneath. Bimota have used bought-in engines throughout most of their history, but fitting a 904cc high compression Ducati motor was probably not that smart a move with hindsight. It's a bit like Ferrari building a concept car for the year 2020, then sticking a hopped up Fiat Bravo engine inside.

But for all its flawed genius, the Tesi is just that – a work of true genius. It could only be an Italian company which had the sheer balls to put something this radical into production. Even Honda, who bought rights to the similar Elf racer project, never got round to making a road version, and Yamaha's GTS 1000cc tourer was so conventional in every other department that few people even noticed it had a funny front end.

It takes style, vision and a strange gleam in the eye to try and push motorcycling onwards into the twenty-first century, shifting some basic engineering beyond strengthened bicycle frames. The Tesi was, and still is, the bravest, most beautiful statement on the subject which ever turned a wheel.

VITAL STATISTICS

Engine: 904cc, water cooled, four stroke, V-twin, eight valve Ducati. **Gears:** six speed. **Carbs:** None, direct Weber fuel injection. **Estimated peak power:** 100bhp @ 8,500rpm.
Frame: Aluminium twin spar, inverted, utilizing engine as stressed member – steel tubular sub-frame.
Front Suspension: Marzocchi monoshock, multi-adjustable, mounted on hub centre steering arrangement, using swinging arm fork and hydraulic steering rack.
Rear Suspension: Swinging arm, Marzocchi monoshock, multi adjustable.
Brakes: Triple Brembo discs, four piston calipers at front.
Estimated Top Speed: 135mph.

Hub-centre steering also featured on the US built Militaire in 1911.

97 500 MACH III TRIPLE

Kawasaki

Best 60s two stroke to scare yourself on

 Kawasaki were the last of the Japanese "Big Four" factories to ship their bikes over to the UK, and after making a few basic mistakes – like copying BSA A10 four stroke twins – they suddenly discovered the berserk world of high performance two strokes.

But two cylinders weren't enough to set them apart from Yamaha, Bridgestone or Suzuki, so Kawasaki's most fiendish engineers came up with a range of terrifying two stroke, three cylinder engines – eventually spanning 250–750cc by the early 70s. The first one was the Mach III, however, and what a smoking, snarling beast it was.

The engine offered no real technical advances over most two strokes of the time, except that it had a separate lube system for the bottom end, rather than running a petrol and oil mix straight from the fuel tank. The basic rule Kawasaki had with these fire-spitting triples was this: squeeze as much fuel and air into the cylinder head as possible, light the spark plug, then stand well back.

The reason for that was two-fold. Firstly, the Mach III accelerated like no other 60s roadbike, exploding through the quarter

VITAL STATISTICS

Engine: 498cc Three cylinder, two stroke. **Gears:** five speed. **Estimated peak power:** 60bhp @ 7,500rpm. **Estimated top speed:** 120mph.

The Mach III's bigger, purple-painted 750cc brother was known as the "Purple People-Eater" in the USA.

mile in a fraction over 13 seconds – as fast as the sensational Honda CB750 four of the same year and kicking sand in the face of every big British twin.

Secondly, it handled like a three-wheeled shopping trolley on ice. The spindly

forks and frame, matched with crudely-sprung shock absorbers at the back, simply couldn't handle an explosion of 60bhp halfway around a corner. It also had totally inadequate brakes.

These bikes were known as "Green Meanies" for very good reasons.

But the sheer adrenaline rush of gunning the 500 triple up through its five gears hooked many bikers for years on Kawasakis, thus establishing a great reputation for almost psychotic performance and evil handling. The fact that it only did about 25mpg, seized up its middle cylinder at the merest speck of carbon on a sparkplug, or turned its chrome into rust if you breathed heavily on it was irrelevant. The Mach III was a kick-ass, pure Tiger-In-Your-Tank, 60s hedonists' delight.

A bike to make you grin, even if it was sometimes in fear...

❝it handled like a three-wheeled shopping trolley on ice❞

■ **A man behaving sadly on the most kick-ass two stroke of the 60s**

12

CBR1000 96

Fastest 80s blancmange on wheels

❝like a turbo-charged Lay-Z-Boy Recliner, styled by Jane Asher❞

■ For some, a lazy 130hp and sedate 160mph will be enough. So Honda do it

When Honda came back to making big across-the-frame four cylinder bikes, which worked, rather then the dodgy VF1000 and VF750 bikes of the early 80s, they learned a lesson from Ford. The dominant mass-production car maker of the twentieth century had stunned Europe a few years earlier with its "jelly mould" styled Sierra range. Despite criticism, the Sierra had gone on to become a sales success by being that bit different in looks, yet being utterly conventional under its Mr Blobby skin. The CBR1000, launched in 1987 alongside its sister bike – the CBR600 – was another rounded, almost pot-bellied sort of motorcycle, but it was blindingly fast and, more importantly, easy as pie to ride. Rivals like the GPZ900R Kawasaki, or GSXR1100 Suzuki demanded much more rider skill to bring out their sporty advantages on the road, but the CBR1000 just whistled quietly along – at 160mph. It was like a turbo-charged Lay-Z-Boy Recliner, styled by Jane Asher.

But for it all its visual blandness, espe-cially in its early white/red or black/red colour combinations, the CBR1000 had a profound impact on big bikes in the late 80s. Manufacturers saw their market shift-ing slowly nearer to middle-aged, middle-management territory, which meant things like rider comfort actually mattered. Here, the CBR really scored, with a plush saddle, raised handlebars, fuel gauge, decent pillion space and soft suspension. A full day on the road wasn't a huge prob-lem on the CBR1000, especially if there was a great deal of motorway mileage included, whereas the rakish lad-about-town on his FZR1000 Yamaha, or big Suzy, would've got off his bike wondering if some joker had replaced the seat with a piece of MFI marble-effect, arse-splitting chip-board.

The CBR1000 also had an engine which was invented for lazy riding, making loads of lowdown power like the FJ1200 Yamaha, with no Kawasaki type "cammi-ness" when you did get round to revving the thing hard. Unlike the Yamaha, the CBR never really overwhelmed its chassis completely at high speed either, there was that discernible feeling of security, pre-dictability even, about the big Honda. It was a giant Durex Safe Play condom. Later models were extensively developed in a failed attempt to present the CBR1000 as some kind of halfway house between the Fireblade and the truly wondrous VFR750, but linked brakes, sharper steering and firmer suspension weren't enough. In any event, the 'Blade itself went almost cud-dly after a couple of years, effectively nicking the CBR1000's market.

No more Mr. Nice Guy.

VITAL STATISTICS

Engine: 998cc water cooled, DOHC, 16 valve, four cylinder, four stroke. Gears: six speed. Dry weight: 235kgs. Estimated peak power: 130bhp @ 9,500rpm. Estimated top speed; 160mph.

Unlike many sports tourers, the CBR1000 has a good range on its 4.8 gallon petrol tank.

95 ZRX1100

Best bad boys burnout bike ever

Just like Eddie's, the Kawasaki ZXR1100 is an unashamed homage to what was surely Kawasaki's finest hour: those big green beasties that Lawson and Rainey used to dominate the Superbike class before someone decided to ban them. Just as well probably. Those race-kitted road bikes were like runaway rhinos and even the hard charging youngbloods who straddled the air-cooled four cylinder behemoths looked like they were just hanging on for dear life most of the time. The big K had started all this retro carry-on with the Zephyr – a machine that mimicked the deeply sexy and quintessentially seventies Z900.

VITAL STATISTICS

Engine: Four cylinder, four stroke air cooled engine. Estimated peak power: 120bhp @ 10,000rpm. Estimated top speed: 130mph. Dry weight: 189kgs. Fuel capacity: 17 litres.

The twin six piston Tokico calipers fitted on the front of the ZRX1100 are powerful enough to punch a hole in the space time continuum and propel you into a parrellel universe.

However, like a public school punk the Zephyr looked the part; street tough and full of spit and swearing but underneath it was... well, as soft as shite. Suzuki then went and got it absolutely correct with the big 1200 Bandit. Born to behave badly it was immediately installed as the weapon of choice for power-crazed hooligans. Fortunately for Kawasaki they already built the motorcycle with more grunt than the triple-X rated re-make of *Babe*: the 180mph ZRX1100.

Installed in the double cradle steel frame, which looks the part even if it is no longer cutting edge, the 1100cc liquid-cooled lump returned around twenty-five fewer ponies but, more significantly the proud bulge of torque remained intact. Straddle a ZRX1100 and every set of lights turns into Santa Pod. The styling is as eighties as The Thomson Twins on *Top of the Pops* from the flat bars and bikini fairing at the front to the piggy-back twin shocks and braced swinging arm at the back. All it's missing is a Kerker pipe and a lick of green, white and blue paint.

> **' more grunt than the triple-X-rated re-make of 'Babe' '**

■ **Every set of traffic lights becomes Santa Pod on a ZXR1100**

RED HUNTER 94

Best sporty single for splendid fellows

Ariel

You don't look at the mantelpiece while you're poking the fire. This statement, intended to cover another area of activity altogether, is equally applicable to motorcycling and just as wrong. An ugly motorcycle is an aberration and will only sell to black-fingered engineering fetishists, muttering eccentrics and the French. No-one has been more aware of this essential truth than Edward Turner and rarely has a motorcycle stirred the loins of sporting chaps so much as his rakish Ariel Red Hunter from the 1930s. Today of course the jobs of engineering and styling are entirely separate, the first usually done by someone with a side parting and an unnatural love of short sleeved shirts, the second by art school types with a deep-seated sexual psychosis. That seems to work best but old Eddie baby was one of a rare breed: he could do all the sums and still make a motorcycle so good you'd elbow your granny out of the way to get a better look.

Ariel were Birmingham-based peddlers of push irons and their tentative excursions into motorcycling were timid creatures. That changed in 1926 when a chap called

> **❝An ugly motorcycle is an aberration and will only sell to black-fingered engineering fetishists, muttering eccentrics and the French❞**

■ **Confusingly, the Red Hunter was also offered in a tasteful Wedgewood blue livery**

VITAL STATISTICS

Engine: 347cc. Four-speed Burman gearbox. Estimated peak power: 17bhp @ 5,600rpm. Estimated top speed: 80 mph. Dry weight: 145kgs.

As well as appearing in commercials, top madcap comedian Vic Reeves is a committed enthusiast of the Ariel marque.

Val Page came up with a 500cc overhead valve single. By the 30s Ariel had escaped their humble origins, bought out Triumph and started production of Turner's rather spiffing Square Four. So it was inevitable that their sporting single would get the Turner treatment. Renamed the Red Hunter and equipped with an engine of either 250, 350 or 500cc and a four speed gearbox, it gained bright paint, high-level pipes and lashings of chrome – and it worked.

Like so many of the legendary names

from the golden years between the wars – Indian, Velocette and now, God help us, Norton – the Ariel name was destined to be dragged through the dirt, appearing on desperate nonsense unworthy of the name. Reading about Turner I thought he had a lot in common with Harley Earl – the uninspired architect of America's auto excess. Both realised they weren't just shifting metal, they were selling dreams and it's ironic that in the year of Earl's iconic '59 Cadillac Ariel made their last machine – a three wheeler moped.

Vive le Rocker

What a bunch of cults. From Mods and Rockers to Hell's Angels and the Harley Owners Group the two-wheeled world has always attracted those seeking an off-the-shelf identity. Today of course it's the scary, snarly world of the streetfighter that's gaining converts quicker than a Death Row priest in a Texas gaol. The look is easy enough; take at least one hundred horsepower's worth of large motorcycle, remove the fairing (this can be done by crashing, or, if you prefer, you can just unbolt it – you loser!) Next, fit flat motorcross bars and an exhaust so loud that if the wind is in the right direction, they can hear you in France. Congratulations! You now have a motorcycle that is slower and handles worse then when you started. Now go and buy yourself a mutant faced Simpson helmet oh, and a bus pass since your driving licence now has the life expectancy of a security officer in an old episode of *Star Trek*. Or you could go for Triumph's T509 Speed Triple. The T509 wants you to think it's a hooligan and it looks the part, in Badass Black or In-Yer-Face Orange with all its bits hanging out in the breeze, except underneath it's actually awfully well-behaved. The engine is a lovely fuel-injected 955cc triple in user-friendly 90bhp guise rather than the user-scary 110hp beasty that lives under

> **❛ buy a bus pass, since your driving licence now has the life expectancy of a security officer in an old episode of *Star Trek*❜**

■ **Big, black and bad**

VITAL STATISTICS

Engine: 955cc triple four stroke water cooled engine. Estimated peak power: 90bhp @ 10,000rpm. Estimated top speed: 130mph. Dry weight: 203kgs. Fuel capacity: 19 litres.

Fact: this bike is a complete wheelie-monster.

the pervy plastic of the gorgeous T595 and supplies a stream of instant creamy urge as long as you keep stomping through the six-speed box. Top speed is a slightly under-whelming 130mph but unless you have the upper body strength of an Orangutan you'll want to keep it well under three figures most of the time. If you do you'll enjoy the ease with which that distinctive tube chassis and single-sided swing arm deal with the available urge and the fun that can be had blasting down B-roads revelling to the gorgeous growl from the three cylinder lump.

Return of the Thumper

When we look at the biking habits of other nations we often do so in the manner of a Sunday evening light entertainment show hosted by the sultan of smirk Clive James. In other words, only doing so to derive amusement from their peculiar and sometimes perverse habits. Americans will only ride a motorcycle bigger than a moose and demand such essentials as reverse gears, flag pole mounting points and panniers spacious enough to accomodate an entire family of Mexican hitch hikers.

The Germans are utterly forbidden to add so much as an oversized mudflap to their machines – this and a diet of sports bikes restricted to 100hp has driven them quite mad and as a result are unnaturally fond of horrible factory customs, BMWs and brown leathers. The French, well, apart from handbag-snatching youths on scooters, its all off-road tackle isn't it? I can't think why the French are quite so keen on long travel suspension and seat heights at groin straining altitude since in my experience most of them are short arses. Still

> **Americans will only ride a motorcycle bigger than a moose and demand such essentials as reverse gears, flag pole mounting points and panniers spacious enough to accomodate an entire family of Mexican hitch hikers**

they are keen on thumping single cyclinder trail machinery and this is the bike which revived that market; the Yamaha XT500. Intoduced in 1977, its best feature was undoubtedly the overhead-camshaft single cylinder motor although the rest of it was commendably uncomplicated and considerably tougher than old boots which tend to be knackered and worn out. In fact the engine was low powered and utilitarian - like the Brit singles of old - yet the XT500 managed to ooze that all important chracteristic; fun.

Light, grunty and ballsy, just the thing for a dirty weekend.

■ Like the old Brit singles, but better made

Rudge

Best Barnstorming Brit single

In 1928, Graham Walker (yes, that's right, Murray's Dad) won the Ulster Grand Prix at an average speed in excess of 80mph. That was a record. What was even more remarkable was that he had won it on a four valve head engined bike, which was something new and obviously powerful. The incredible fact is, however, that despite the racing advantage which Rudge-Whitworth demonstrated in 1928, and then again most spectacularly at the 1930 TT, when they won the Senior and Junior (250cc class) events with four valve singles, few other manufacturers took the technology seriously.

There was nothing fundamentally new in the Rudge Ulster's 499cc engine casings of course, because the demands of the First World War had pushed aircraft engineering to its limits on a daily basis, as the struggle for survival acted as a catalyst in petrol engine design. Four valve heads were par for the course in aeroplanes by the early 1920s.

Rudge were chasing a dream – to make the finest, fastest, roadgoing singles. Their engine boasted a unique pent-roof combustion chamber, with the radially set exhaust valves giving better top end gasflow to the twin exhaust pipes. An ingenious rocker arm arrangement, aluminium-bronze cylinder head and pressed up, roller bearing crankshaft made it leading edge technology for the time.

The only criticism you could level at the engine was that it still retained pushrods rather than overhead camshafts driven by gears, and that the valve gear was still exposed. Despite lubrication, it wore out quickly as the weather, dirt, starving street urchins and other 1930s obstacles collided with the engine.

■ **Pedal that metal: Rudge started off in life as bicycle builders**

Rudge had a wealth of experience building transmissions – they were famous for the Rudge Multi, featuring a variable belt-drive arrangement, bit like a Daf car, if you've ever had the personal misery of driving such an abomination – so it shouldn't have come as a surprise to any buyer that the Rudge Ulster had an in-house designed, four speed gearbox. Foot change was introduced from 1932 onwards.

Technically, the Rudge Ulster was way ahead of its time, but that was the trouble. When the stock market crash of 1929 in the USA started throwing millions onto the dole in the early 30s, the precision built motorcycle had to give way to more basic transportation. Rudge were still winning road racing glory, and notable speedway success, but the financial writ-

ing was on the wall. In 1933, the receivers were called in.

Strangely enough, the Rudge-Whitworth concern was eventually bought up in 1935 by EMI, the electrical giant, who continued some sort of production at the Coventry factory, where Rudge had started out in the nineteenth century making bicycles. There were sporadic race victories still, but the great days of Rudge dominance were over. Other great singles, like the Excelsior Manxman and the "cammy" Norton, were just that bit better and, although Rudge had made their engine better, with enclosed valve gear and a full radial head design, it wasn't a world-beater anymore.

It was, however, a great bike, with a blueprint for the future encapsulated within its fiery engine. Smaller, lighter valves, in better breathing twin port single cylinder engines sap less of the energy within the combustion chamber – that means more power gets to the rear wheel, simple as that.

When production of war equipment meant EMI stopped making Rudges, another opportunity to provide advanced, fuel efficient engineering in the post-war period died with it. Crude, cheap, side-valve BSA, Triumph and Norton products were the bread and butter of War Department production, which in turn became the clattering, antique, unreliable piles of old pants which the factories tried to foist onto a ration book-fondling public from 1945 onwards.

Never again would cheerful blokes in flat hats announce – for no particular sane reason – "Don't Trudge It, Rudge It!" Great slogan.

■ **Rudge actually returned to push-bike production after going bust building motorbikes**

‟Rudge were chasing a dream – to make the finest, fastest, roadgoing singles❞

Henderson

Best American bike that's not a V-twin

Three hundred and forty. Believe it or not that is number of private individuals or transglobal corporations that have managed to stick their name on the side of what we in the free world call a motorcycle within the closely-watched boundaries of The United States of America. Now, try and name them. I'll wager one was easy (Harley-D) two was kinda tricky (Indian) and three well, unless you're reading this in the comfortable confines of the Dunbikin' Rest Home for Vintage and Veteran Motorcyclists, I very much doubt you'll recall the glory days of American marques like Wagner, Thor or Pierce and you probably think Flying Merkel was one of the attractions down at Barnum and Baileys. Strangely it wasn't the depression of the thirties that killed them off but the affluence of the roaring twenties. By the time of the Wall Street Crash in 1929 Detroit had churned out 25 million cars to clog the roads of America. Perhaps the saddest and most ironic casualty was a fantastic four cylin

Fourmidable: First built in 1912, William Henderson's 4 cylinder was still being built, by Indian, in 1942

der bike – built in the motor city itself – the Henderson 4.

William G Henderson had a dream. It involved a bath full of thousand island dressing and the primary schoolteacher who lived next door, but he also had another dream of a smooth and powerful motorcycle with an in-line four cylinder engine. However when the first Henderson 4 appeared in 1912 it was clear that as well as having one rather excellent idea i.e. the four cylinder 8 hp engine, old Bill and brother Tom had some pretty bizarre ones too, like giving his bike a super-long 65 inch wheel base – a practice later adopted by Greyhound for their buses – and placing the pillion in front of the rider with footrests on the front wheel spindle. Perhaps the only time in American motorcycling history when one of those stickers that say 'No Fat Chicks' has been a safety measure rather than a bad ass lifestyle statement.

Henderson was bought out by Schwinn, who made bicycles (and still do), and moved to Chicago. They stuck with the Henderson name and in 1927 produced the wonderfully handsome and thoroughly modern looking motorcycle. Its 1300cc four with improved cooling (because keeping the back cylinders at operating temperature was always a problem with this configuration) gave around 40 hp and made it good for the magic 100mph. But Bill never got to see it, he left the company in 1919 and was killed testing another four cylinder machine, the Ace, in 1922; the Henderson name disappeared in 1931. If you can't imagine yourself astride one of these roaring twenties superbikes clad in leather jacket and jodhpurs thundering down a dirt road determined to get a swift one in down the speakeasy before last orders then you don't deserve to call yourself a motorcyclist...

VITAL STATISTICS

Engine: in-line air-cooled four cylinder 920cc 28hp **Top speed:** 60 mph (1912) 1300cc, 40hp, 100mph (1929)
The Henderson name reappeared on a new bike at Daytona Bike Week in 1998. A new company called Excelsior Henderson announced they had raised $60 million and machines would be ready by late '98. However, both of their prototypes had v-twin engines rather than the legendary in line four.

> ❝William G Henderson had a dream. It involved a bath full of thousand island dressing and the primary schoolteacher who lived next door❞

MONKEY 89

Fabbest and grooviest fun bike for swinging sixties hipsters

Why Monkey? Well, some people said you had to be bananas to buy one (or was that nuts?) But other people, who weren't irritating tossers, knew that these bonsai bikes were so named because in Japan our closest cousins in the animal kingdom are associated with good luck. As with most things, the Japanese had borrowed someone else's idea and made it pay. Folding motorcycles had been around since the Second World War, when they were parachuted into the front line. Although with tiny wheels (castors really) their principal use must have been to make the

VITAL STATISTICS

Engine: 50cc single cylinder four stroke air cooled engine.
Estimated peak power: 6bhp @ 8,000rpm.
Estimated top speed: 35mph.
Dry weight: 65kgs.

Although the smallest bike on the road, the Monkey got its name not from it's size – or it would have been called the Honda Gerbil – but because primates are considered to be good luck.

export to the decadent west has become an obsession with the Japanese whose economic miracle has enabled them to indulge their often-eccentric whims. There are magazines dedicated to the cult of the Monkey, bursting with choice tuning kits from Yoshimura big-bores to titanium exhausts systems. In fact I rode a Monkey, fully tricked up with all the tackle, at 75mph at which point it hit a bump and went into lock-to-lock slapper. How I laughed as I tried to cheat death aboard this comedic contraption.

> **❛it looked less like a motorcycle and more like a wheeled thermos flask – but it worked a treat❜**

enemy laugh so he couldn't aim straight.

In civvy street, most people didn't have to be parachuted into work or dodge enemy shelling on the way back from the Co-op, so the mini bike soon disappeared from the showroom. In the swinging sixties Honda recycled the concept and managed to convince decadent westerners that the Monkey was like a two-wheeled Mini Moke. The marketing was choc full of blokes in blazers stood on yachts waving to cheerleader types with perfect teeth and big beach balls. A tiny thing painted red with a tartan seat, it looked less like a motorcycle and more like a wheeled thermos flask, but it worked a treat and Honda have been selling them ever since. In 1972 they released the Gorilla, a bigger Monkey (geddit?) with a 50cc engine, still with a three-speed gearbox.

Almost inevitably, a vehicle intended for

■ **The nature of Monkey was... irrepressible. Steady sellers since the 60s, they are still popular**

VENOM THRUXTON

Velocette

500 Great Eccentric Bike

■ Velos had great names – all but the '31 KTT, known as the Whiffing Clara!

Veloce Ltd were founded in 1905 by Johann Goodman and, in one of those typical sagas of our once proud British industry, the descendants of the Goodman family presided over the eventual bankruptcy of Velocette in 1971. Like so many other key people in the motorcycle industry, they couldn't – or wouldn't – listen to calls for change. Essentially, they lived in a Victorian timewarp, where men with sensible side-partings debated the merits of mag-dyno ignition over tea and digestives – the biscuits being the better electrical system by far, of course...

But along the way, Velocette made some great bikes, and the Venom Thruxton was perhaps the very best of them. The Thruxton was a celebration of racetrack success, and record breaking speed runs at Montlhery, launched in 1965, refined the original overhead valve engined Venom to a rakish, glorious peak. With its racy half fairing, raunchy clear plastic headlight cover

the choice of the pedantic, the perverse, or the just plain crazy

and adjustable rear shock mountings, the Thruxton was a boy racer's dream.

Being complete eccentrics, however, Velocette retained ancient electrics – which were generally prone to total failure should a sparrow breathe heavily on the wiring. There was also a strange clutch, which worked as part of the final drive mechanism, and the 30s style "fishtail" silencer on the end of the exhaust. In a nutshell, the Venom – or almost any Velocette for that matter – was the choice of the pedantic, the perverse, or the just plain crazy.

But in the Venom Thruxton, the faults fade into the background as your eye sweeps across that beautiful black and gold engineering statement. There's a certain

symmetry, a discernible balance in the lines of the Velo, and every part of it barks speed from a long-forgotten era.

By the mid 60s, no ancient OHV 500cc four stroke single had a right to be in any sort of demand, as the Japanese started selling their faster, more reliable lightweight 125s and 250s – bikes which were almost as fast, despite being half the size. But the Venom had class, the sort of charisma that made grown men take up smoking St Bruno and attach leather patches to their tweed jackets. It oozed tradition like a Hovis advert, and plenty of motorcyclists aspired to own something so rare, so raucous, even if they could only afford a hideous BSA 250 and a "Fab" ice lolly.

When the Velocette works in Birmingham closed, the individuality which had made British bikes the best – and the worst – in the world at one time died with it.

VITAL STATISTICS

**Engine: 499cc, four stroke, air cooled, OHV, single cylinder.
Gears: 4 speed. Estimated peak power: 36bhp @ 6,200rpm.
Estimated top speed: 110mph.**

Velocette got their name because dealers in the 1920s usually added the suffix 'ette' to identify a small capacity bike from a manufacturer. So Veloce Ltd. became Velocette.

NORDWEST 600  87

Best French bike built in Italy

Gilera

■ **Go Nordwest my son... but mind yourself on the petrol tank**

The French. An odd lot I think you'll agree. Eating garden pests, kissing blokes, standing room only in the smallest room – but nowhere is their obstinate eccentricity better demonstrated than in the arena of motorcycle sport. For a start there's the Paris Dakar – which doesn't start in Paris or finish in Dakar, but that sums up the essence of riding an out-sized off-roader at three figure speeds across a scorching featureless desert for days on end without getting lost or killed. Then there's supermotard where switching from tarmac to grass isn't followed by an ambulance ride and a pethidine drip but an essential part of a sport that demands hybrid bikes with on-and-off road attributes and riders who can likewise swing both ways, usually with an outstretched boot skimming the surface, the front end eating air and the throttle wound back to the stop.

Full-on French-bloke Jean Michel Bayle was perhaps the ultimate exponent of this full-on approach and was worshiped as a god. Still, as the French motorcycle indus-

try had been reduced to a dozen snail-scoffers, nailing moped engines to the front wheel of robust bicycles it took the Italians to come up with a supermotard spin-off for the street. The Gilera Nordwest was just the job for hot-blooded Mediterranean types who used the instant 55hp surge of that big 4-valve single to annihilate Uno Turbos in the traffic light Grand Prix. The lack of lard and flighty upside-down front end means big wheelies on demand while the killer front stopper twin disc and four piston callipers mean crushing your testicles against an unyielding metal object was never easier. The name didn't hurt either, Gilera being legendary builders of single-cylinder road and race bikes. If you were interested in more than impressing the teen queens of the local *trattoria* then the Nordwest could hold its own in fairly serious four cylinder company using its blinding brakes and long travel suspension to tackle the crumbling causeways that pass for roads in southern Europe. The Gilera Nordwest was the Toyota RV4 of the bike world and I mean that in the nicest way.

❛annihilate Uno Turbos in the traffic light Grand Prix❜

VITAL STATISTICS

Engine: 600cc single cylinder four valve, four stroke
Engine output: 55bhp@6,000rpm
Gears: five.

Gilera, the oldest of Italy's motorcycling marques stopped building bikes in the sixties but the name was acquired by the giant Piaggio concern, best known as makers of Vespa scooters.

86 CB400F

Best baby four cylinder bike

There were four cylinder bikes before this one, but the Honda 400 Four was a compact masterpiece. For the Quo-loving, Peter Stuyvesant-smoking, flared Brutus jeans generation of the 70s, this motorcycle was probably their first "proper" bike, following a painful apprenticeship on a collection of rancid two strokes.

At heart, it was a slimmed-down version of the single overhead cam 1969 Honda CB750, with four carbs, six gears and an incredibly gorgeous exhaust system, which rippled like a river of chrome, away to the right hand side of the machine. Most of all, it had a uniquely understated style about it, being only available in blue or red at first, which in an era featuring such fashion nightmares as the Rubettes in matching suits and berets was no bad thing.

Mind you, Honda did make a version of the F2 model in a colour called Parakeet Yellow.

On top of that, the smallest incarnation of the Honda fours (apart from the short-lived 350cc version which never made it into the UK) was the best handling of them, too. A simple cradle chassis, cheap shocks and basic telescopic forks shouldn't have set it apart from its competition, but somehow the power characteristics of the buzzy 400cc motor never overwhelmed the bend-swinging abilities of the bike.

The result was a bike which allowed fairly new bikers to build up confidence rather than pitching them into the nearest hedge at 80mph as many a Suzuki or Kawasaki triple did…

The only weaknesses the Honda had were in the carbs department, where a flat spot the size of Lincolnshire made mid-range acceleration pretty dismal, and the feeble front disc brake, which appeared to be made of teak utilizing plasticene brake pads. Back then, even Honda weren't perfect.

Although it was a runaway success in Britain, the 400 Four proved unpopular elsewhere, particularly in the States, so Honda pulled the plug after just two years of production, turning the 400 Four into an instant classic.

VITAL STATISTICS

Engine: 408cc four cylinder, SOHC, four stroke, air cooled. Gears: six speed. Dry weight: 397lbs. Estimated peak power: 37bhp @ 8,500rpm. Estimated top speed: 100mph.

Early models had pillion footpegs mounted directly on the swing-arm, so passengers had to have quite bendy knees on rough roads … or get used to torn ligaments.

> **❝an incredibly gorgeous exhaust system which rippled like a river of chrome❞**

■ **Fantastic Four: Soichiro Honda, the genius of modern motorcycling, often said that the smooth and sweet-holding 400/4 was his favourite motorbike**

KR1S 250 85

Best bike behaving badly ■

ooliganism. Every generation thinks they invented it and they're wrong, except I suppose Mr Hooligan. If ever there was a bike you should never buy second hand it is the Kawasaki KR1S, motorcycling's two-fingered salute to straight society. There was only one reason anyone ever bought this bike: because it was fast, loud and cheap. Yes, the two-stroke twin would eventually explode into a million pieces but it was worth it for the anti-social activity it engendered while it held together. If you were brave enough then this badly behaved little bike would scream its way to 12,000rpm and a top speed that was a gnat's knob under 140mph. I can think of no other motorcycle where each and every one of the Silkolene-sniffers who bought one will have made a concerted effort to attain that top speed. It's a Kawasaki, so of course it's all about the engine: 55 horsepower of liquid-cooled, reed-valve assisted psychopathic intensity; the

■ **A screaming Dinky toy on steroids**

> ❝It's a Kawasaki so of course it's all about the engine: 55 horsepower of liquid-cooled, reed-valve assisted psychopathic intensity; the Ronnie and Reggie Kray of parallel twins.❞

Ronnie and Reggie Kray of parallel twins.

Naturally, it didn't handle. The chassis and suspension were as basic and primitive as Welsh fertility rituals and even more scary. The big problem was the brakes: discs all round with twin, four pot calipers up front, they were just too good. With the dry weight of an empty crisp packet the KR1S was quite capable of getting you into more trouble than an unexpected itemised phone bill and adrenaline junkies loved it for that very reason. The other thing that made it such a belting road bike was the size. It was made to fit an organ grinder when Honda and Suzuki tailored the dimensions of their 250s to the monkey. You know what I said at the start, well forget

it. You can pick one of these things up for the price of a half-decent push-bike – each one you see advertised will claim an existence of scrupulous servicing and on-the-road restraint, which is, of course, bollocks.

Sort the suspension and swap the unfashionable rubber for state of the art grippy stuff and I reckon you've got the perfect track day weapon for embarrassing Born Agains on 'Blades.

The KR1S is speed in a pure concentrated form; take it three times a day.

VITAL STATISTICS

Engine: 250cc, two-stroke liquid cooled tandem twin
Power output: 55bhp @ 11,100 rpm.
Gears: six.
Dry Weight 131kgs
Top Speed (estimated): 138mph.

At one stage in the late eighties half the grid in almost every UK 250 race were on KR1S machines.

84 Cagiva MITO 125

The 916 for rich kids

If you were the spoilt bastard boy offspring of some currency trading vulture in the early 1990s, there was no finer piece of motorcycle one-upmanship than the Cagiva Mito 125. Styled by Tamburini himself, echoing the sumptuous Ducati 916 in all the right places, the seven speed Cagiva was a screaming brat out of teenage hell. Beautiful, yet unattainable. Like sexual relations with the most stunning sixth former, or automatic entry to the hippest nightclub in town, the Cagiva Mito was always tantalizingly just out of reach. Well actually, it was ridiculously

With its close ratio seven speed gearbox that could take a determined thrasher to the naughty side of 100mph, at which point the pistons would explode through your rectum – no, only joking, it was dead reliable.

Honest.

Anyway, did that humble performance matter when a bike could look so stunning, so very close to a real 125 GP bike? With its banana shaped swingarm (on the

VITAL STATISTICS

Engine: 124cc single cylinder, water cooled, two stroke. Gears: seven speed. Carburettor: 28mm Dell Orto. Estimated peak power; 33bhp @ 10,000rpm. Chassis: Aluminium beam frame, 40mm upside down Marzocchi forks, multi-adjustable Boge monoshock rear. Dry weight; 125kgs. Brakes: Single 320mm Brembo front disc. Estimated top speed: 105mph.

The Mito has exactly the same mirrors as fitted to the Ducati 916 or Bimota SB6R.

> **Like sexual relations with the most stunning sixth former, or automatic entry to the hippest nightclub in town, the Cagiva Mito was always tantalisingly just out of reach**

■ Sad GCSE question: You're seventeen, and you can have a Mito or a second-hand Vauxhall Nova...

beyond the means of your average burger flipper or routinely abused trainee exhaust fitter. But that's not to say the Mito was some bit of outrageous, impractical Italian froth with no use whatsoever. It could be easily de-restricted from its feeble UK spec 12bhp and boosted to an altogether more acceptable 33bhp output.

Evolutione model), three spoke Marchesini wheels, Marzocchi upside forks and multi-adjustable Boge monoshock, the Mito was pure hotshot class in miniature. A road scalpel. You could drink in details like the exact replica Ducati 916 headlights, the horizontally mounted steering damper, the gold anodized Brembo brake carrier

and matching four piston caliper. A thing of exquisite expense is never dull, boring commuter tackle; riding a Mito was – still is – an event, a completely over the top pose for some manic staring runt in scuffed leathers with a point to prove, a boy racer who never grew up. If there's a bit of the kid in all bikers, then there's a place in motorcycling for the Cagiva Mito.

NR750

Honda's V8 engined motorcycle

 When Honda failed to make their NR500 four stroke GP bike a competitive reality, they packed it up and stuck it in the backroom at H.Q. for the boys to play with. The NR project was always a complex, experimental solution to by-pass the F.I.M. ruling forbidding the use of more than four cylinders in a racing bike engine, so the engineers began to think of a way to make V8 power from the oval piston four cylinder layout. They spent most of the 1980s refining and re-building their various prototypes, gaining knowledge and power via endurance racing, until they released a spaceship styled concept bike which stunned onlookers with its craftsmanship and technology. Oddly, Honda opted to offer just 125bhp, developed at a banshee wailing 14,000rpm, when pre-production models had made over 150bhp without too much trouble. The secret of all this extra potential power lies in the unique oval pistons. Shaped like tins of Spam, the piston crowns have enough surface area to squeeze eight valves, almost brushing their tops, with twin titanium conrods supporting each piston. Gear driven cams are the only option on something this potent, with some cast magnesium cases to keep engine weight reasonable, Nikasil lined cylinders for heat dissipation, plus two spark plugs per cylinder. Two curved radiators keep the massive unit cool and the engine is fed by fuel injection, with a four into two stainless steel exhaust system exiting under the tailpiece.

With carbon fibre details and its Ferrari inspired body panels, the NR750 is still a fantastically good looking bike; in fact you can see how some might argue that Tamburini was more than slightly influ-

---

VITAL STATISTICS

Engine: 748cc, V4 cylinder, DOHC, 32 valve, water cooled, four stroke. **Gears:** six speed. **Carbs:** none, eight way fuel injection. **Estimated peak power:** 125bhp @ 14,000rpm. **Chassis:** Aluminium beam frame, 45mm upside down forks, rising rate monoshock. **Dry weight:** 225kgs. **Estimated top speed:** 165mph.

Niall Mackenzie raced one and owns a roadgoing NR750.

---

enced by the Honda when he penned the Ducati 916. The bottom line with the NR750, however, was price; £37,000 on the road, back in 1992 – when new bike sales were in their worst slump for 10 years – just wasn't a viable option for all but the super rich eccentrics and collectors. The other downer about the NR was its weight. At 225 kgs, it was heavier than more mundane motorcycles like Bimotas, Fireblades, OWO1 Yamahas etc. All that pork made it relatively slow, especially in terms of acceleration,

compared to the Fireblade 900. People marvelled at Honda's technological feat – they had made the infamous "Nearly Ready" project a viable proposition, but it was too much money and five years too late. A tragedy.

Why? Because motorcycling needs bold statements, pure acts of engineering, to push us forwards along the road.

> **With carbon fibre details and its Ferrari-inspired body panels, the NR750 is still a fantastically good looking bike**

■ **Not many a-round: Honda only allocated five oval-pistoned NR750s for the UK**

Suzuki 82 RG500

Best impression of Barry Sheene's bike

Who do you think you are sonny, Barry Sheene?" Every sad, predictable, radar-toting copper in the 80s must've uttered those words a thousand times, as they issued another backdoor government road tax notice – sorry, speeding ticket – to a keen motorcyclist. The fact is, if you really wanted to look and sound like Bazza

> ❝The whole bike will twitch, wobble and squirm its way through corners at the sort of lean angles which few riders should attempt without fitting stabilisers❞

on the open road, then there was only one choice in 1985; the Suzuki RG500. Like the 1976/77 world champion's own race machine, it was a square four layout, two stroke missile, with a cassette style six speed gearbox, an ultra lightweight twin beam alloy framed chassis and a dinky 16 inch front wheel. Naturally it didn't have quite so much power; a mere 95bhp lurked inside the crackling engine, but the entire motorcycle only weighed 340lbs – slightly less than a Honda 250 Superdream. Oh my lord...

Apart from having about 50bhp less than Bazza's 1984 season racer, the RG500 wasn't radically different for road use. The two stroke engine utilized disc valve induction, drank petrol at a ridiculous rate and was desperately sensitive to bodged attempts at tuning. A handful of maestros in the UK like Stan Stephens in Kent, or Frank Wrathall in Lancashire were – and still are – capable of extracting insane amounts of power from the RG500, but it's the sort of experience that's best sampled on the racetrack. Why? Simple really. Even in stock 95bhp trim, the RG500 will catapult you towards the next village once the rev counter touches 7,000rpm, hoisting the front wheel and taking your breath away. The whole bike will twitch, wobble and squirm its way through corners at the sort of lean angles which few riders should attempt with-

out fitting stabilisers – not because it's a poor handler, but because the power delivery is violent. As in Mike Tyson ears-for-dinner violent.

That Suzuki, Yamaha (RD500) and Honda (NS400) all had the corporate bottle in the mid-80s to release GP technology in a sanitized fashion to the motorcycling public was amazing. But the RG500 was simply the very best of the three machines. Light, agile, ballistic acceleration, decent brakes and reliable for as much as ... oh, 400 miles. Totally impractical for anything except proddie racing, expensive to buy and run, indifferently finished. Yep, Suzuki pulled off a miracle back in 1985; they made a great, glorious, completely beserk bike which could've passed as an Italian. Bravo Bazza.

■ **Brut Force: Nowadays, only Bimota dare offer a 500cc GP replica stroker for prod use – and they don't even race in Grand Prix**

The last of the great British singles

Think about this one piece of motorcycling trivia for a moment: in 1970, Tommy Robb – who now runs a motorbike shop in Warrington – managed to finish 4th in the World 500cc Championship, as a privateer, on a Seeley-Matchless G50 single.

Just imagine the effort involved in competing against explosive two stroke twins, the mighty MV Agusta fours and everyone else, whilst riding a machine which was essentially as basic, spartan and pure as a Manx Norton from 1930. Incredible.

The Matchless G50 started life as part of the AMC company's survival strategy in the late 1950s, following a patchy works racing effort with the G45 four stroke twin. AMC needed some glory to enliven their dull, plodding commuter reputation. The G50 was a step back to the company's roots and drew heavily on the 1948 350cc AJS 7R for inspiration. A 500cc, re-worked 7R engine was the only real difference between these two motorcycles, and both the Ajay and the Matchless G50 competed at the highest levels in road-

> **"thundering along to the chequered flag, ridden by men with balls of steel"**

racing for the next 10 years or so, with riders like Phil Read and Bill Ivy grabbing top three places on them.

But the true purpose of both the AJS and Matchless singles was as the ideal "clubman's" racer. The G50 remained a beautifully simple, OHC, two valve engine unit throughout its lifespan, with plenty of lightweight alloy parts and an inherent toughness which helped it survive regular ham-

■ **Righteous Roadracer: To comply with US racing regs Matchless built fifty G50 street bikes**

merings as riders struggled to keep pace with more modern machinery. It also provided motive power for grass-track, scrambler and sidecar racers, in events where British pluck, a big single and a packet of Capstan Full Strength could often win the day.

Following AMC's financial meltdown in the mid-60s, people like Colin Seeley, Tom Arter (no, I'm not making thse names up) and Tom Kirby all ran race teams which kept the Matchless G50 running hard and fast with the best of them. By the close of the swinging 60s, the writing was on the wall for big four stroke singles, yet a talented racer like Peter Williams could still take the flag in the frighteningly fast North West 200 over in Northern Ireland in 1969.

AMC probably sold fewer than 300 G50 models during the early 60s, but the Matchless marque gained a much-needed sheen of racing glory on the back of it. The great thing about it is that you can visit almost any classic bike racing meeting today and still hear these big, booming singles thundering along to the chequered flag, ridden by men with balls of steel.

They don't want to look at G50s in some museum, or drool over a pristine, Solvol-polished specimen owned by an anally retentive dentist from Leamington Spa. They want to win.

PAN-EUROPEAN

ST1100   Trans-European express

Honda

For years, the Germans, in the shape of BMW, had the touring motorcycle market wrapped up. Their dull, tractor-like flat twins weren't fast, but they were capable of transporting two people, plus luggage, from Accrington to Austerlitz without mechanical disaster.

Then Honda launched the Gold Wing, which changed everything. However, some bikers found the gross laden weight of a Foden truck rather too much when it came to cornering, so the Gold Wing never appealed to the touring rider who actually knew how to take a bend at speeds above 40mph.

But Honda had a secret weapon, and in 1990 the Pan-European ST1100 hit the autobahns to a well-deserved round of applause. Here was a motorcycle with a V4 shaped engine capable of hitting 150mph in a straight line, yet a skilled rider could stuff it into a bend at high speeds and be reasonably confident of emerging in one piece on the other side. It also had a car type shaft final drive, an excellent fairing, plus hard panniers as standard. Grand touring had arrived for executive motorcyclists.

Over the last few years the Pan-Handle – as it's known to most bikers who have never ridden it – has evolved into possibly the most competent all-round, trans-European express. It now has traction control to prevent skids – handy when the bike weighs over 630lbs dry, because you will not save this mothership by sticking your leg out to keep it upright.

VITAL STATISTICS

Engine: 1084cc, water cooled, transverse mounted, V-4 cylinder, four stroke. Gears: five speed. Estimated peak power: 100bhp @ 7,500rpm. Brakes: ABS, plus Honda linked system. Fuel capacity: 6.1 gallons. Estimated top speed: 150mph.

The ST1100 fuel tank is a dummy – the fuel is kept under the seat to keep the weight as low as possible.

It also boasts ABS braking, just like a top class BMW, or a seriously fast luxury motor car. The fairing has been re-designed too, in an attempt to counteract the bike's sensitivity to sidewinds at speed.

Honda are like that – they will not rest until each concept they choose to apply in motorcycling has been refined to the ultimate degree. In the Pan-European, they've created a Parker-Knoll recliner with a jet turbine smooth engine. It never goes wrong, it is effortless to ride, all day, every day. The only thing which makes the Pan deeply uncool for most motorcyclists with red blood in their veins is that it is the preferred choice of police and AA patrolmen – the kiss of death in street cred.

But otherwise, the ST1100 is the only bike which outdoes BMW at their own game – faster, more comfortable and even more clinically soulless. So good, it's spooky.

> **the preferred choice of police and AA patrolmen – the kiss of death in street cred**

■ 'Oi, Gary Rothwell, No!' The ST1100 now features burn-out-proof traction control

Definitive 70s scratcher

Yamaha

Yamaha have always known how to make exciting two strokes. Even today, their TZR250 is one of the most demanding and fiercely fast pocket-sized motorcycles you can obtain. Back in 1976 at the Amsterdam Bike Show they stunned almost everyone with this machine, which soon became the first choice for any boy racer with cash in his flares and a point to prove on the next roundabout.

The RD400 was the culmination of a decade-long search for the ultimate road-going two stroke. The YDS7 and RD250 machines were great learner bikes, but only good for 90mph flat on the tank. The old YR5 and early 70s RD350 were good, but the 398cc RD400 was one of those pieces of clinically precise technology that only come along a couple of times in a manufacturer's lifetime.

With an explosive power delivery above 6,000 revs, a taut frame and suspension package, good ground clearance, decent braking and a similar dry weight to its 250cc cousin, the RD400 was pure, white-line cocaine – a fast rider could easily humble Kawasaki Z1s, Honda 750s or anything else on the right sort of road. The RD quickly became a byword for proddie racers who recognized the hidden power in its elegant simplicity.

Through its four year life-span, it got electronic ignition, more ground clearance, matt black engine paint and a few other minor improvements, but remained a total headbanger's bike – an invitation to a speeding ticket. In truth, the RD400 wasn't that fast, only pulling a genuine top speed in its sixth gear overdrive of around 105mph, but it seemed to get there

VITAL STATISTICS

Engine: 398cc, two stroke, twin cylinder, air cooled. Gears: six speed. Dry weight: 345lbs. Estimated peak power: 44bhp @ 7,500rpm. Estimated top speed: 105mph.

The RD400 was the first production machine to have cast wheels and self-cancelling indicators.

much quicker than any of its rivals. Plus, with some judicious tuning work, a "ported and jetted" RD400 could be persuaded to crack 120mph – without a fairing. A single overhead cam model Honda 750 couldn't match that in 1976.

Of course, it then drank petrol and two stroke oil, vibrated so badly that it could crack a smile on the face of Princess Margaret, and the engine would probably go bang within 1,000 miles at those sort of speeds, but who cared?

The RD400 was a bad boy's toy, a little screamer, the devil in disguise. Although Yamaha had a corporate emblem celebrating their musical instrument heritage, suddenly everyone understood what the tuning fork was really there for.

> **'a bad boy's toy, a little screamer, the devil in disguise'**

■ The RD400 was in production for four years – three times the life expectancy of most of its owners

SPEED TWIN 500

Triumph

The classic British twin

■ In the 60s, Turner designed a 350cc OHC parallel twin - codenamed Bandit – to compete with Japanese bikes

Edward Turner was a genius.

The young designer of the Ariel Red Hunter single and the innovative – but flawed – Ariel Square Four was appointed top man at Triumph in the mid-30s (when he was of a similar age) and he made the company the most successful motorcycle manufacturer in the world over the next 30 years. Not only was Turner a great engineer, but he was a shrewd marketeer too, adding chrome panels, a lick of paint and an evocative name to make a bike a sales success – even if it was the same old plodding hack off the production line as last year.

The Speed Twin of 1937, however, was something special. In fact, if one engine design can be said to define British motorcycles, then this is it. A relatively simple parallel four stroke twin, featuring a 360 degree firing order and a pressed up crankshaft, with a central flywheel slotted between the two halves, it was cheap to produce and powerful. It was also marginally lighter than the typical 500cc single

> *encapsulated all that was good about the motorcycle in the 30s*

cylinder engine of the times.

For his £75 in 1938, a young gadabout with an eye for the ladies got a stunning machine finished in Amaranth Red – quite a novelty when many bikes were still painted black – which could comfortably cruise all day at 60mph, with the occasional burst of furious riding producing a top speed of around 90mph. Heady stuff... then war broke out and the very real danger of having a 1,000lb bomb dropped on your house by the Luftwaffe made motorcycling seem fairly safe.

What the Speed Twin offered was solid, all round performance in a stylish package. Whatever exotic machinery you might have

dreamt of in the 1930s, 40s or 50s, the Triumph twins probably gave you all you would ever need in a bike. The Speed Twin was so good that, following the Second World War, the remaining British factories inevitably copied the parallel twin formula just to stay in business.

The Norton Dommie, BSA A7 Star model, Matchless G80 and Royal Enfield 500 twin all arrived in the 50s and spawned a range of bigger, less reliable, more vibratory range of big British twins which were easy prey for the Japanese invaders in the 60s. The parallel twin became a design blind alley which no large British manufacturer could escape except through bankruptcy.

But let's celebrate Turner's achievement nevertheless, for in one beautiful, versatile machine, he encapsulated all that was good about the motorcycle in the 30s and offered a unique blueprint for the future.

VITAL STATISTICS

Engine: 499cc, pushrod activated OHV, air cooled. Gears: four speed. Estimated peak power: 27bhp @ 6,500rpm. Estimated top speed: 90mph.

Turner for the worse: Eddy baby didn't get it wrong very often, but in 1962 he unleashed the 100cc Tina scooter – and it was crap.

350 SPORT 77

The prettiest star ■

Motorcycling is a broad church and incorporates individuals who, in less enlightened company, would be ostracised, ridiculed and quite possible beaten to death with heavy agricultural implements. I have met a great many of these people, and whether their enthusiasm was for turbo and nitrous-injected BMW boxers, Post Office delivery bikes of the 1950s or even a diesel-engined Enfield, I have managed to see why perhaps they have taken the road less travelled – even if in the oil-burning Enfield's case that was the bus lane – but I could never understand why some people just love the Moto Morini 350cc.

I mean what's that all about, eh? A tiny little 350cc v-twin with weird flat cylinder heads and the combustion chamber in the top of the piston. Electronic ignition, drum brakes, and a six-speed gearbox. Agreed it was the only six-speed four stroke of its time, but for most that was just the answer to a trivial pursuit question that nobody had bothered to ask.

■ **Undeniably gorgeous, it was also twice the price of an RD400**

No, back in the heady days of the early seventies motorcyclists were hungry for the cheap thrills offered by Japan or if they were hirsute of face and wearers of waxed-cotton underwear then they would concur that real men didn't ride anything that small unless it was for charity. Too slow for scratching, too small for touring and too bloody expensive by half – we never understood the little Morini and over here it sold like kosher Christmas cards. The truth is that the Morini 350cc was a cracking little all-rounder with sweet handling, sporty performance and styling that still looks fresh twenty-five years on, but we just did not get it. We didn't get it for the same reason we don't understand cheese for breakfast, hurling livestock off the top of churches and going to bed in the afternoon and not having sex.

We like big bikes and we buy big bikes. Its a cultural thing but it doesn't make us bad people. The factory tried desperately to flog it in a designer suit of bodywork as the Dart model, or the Kanguro trailbike option too. But it didn't work; the Morini was too pretty and too small.

VITAL STATISTICS

Engine: 344cc v-twin four stroke air cooled. Estimated peak power: 40bhp @ 8,500rpm. Estimated top speed: 105mph. Dry weight: 153kgs. Fuel capacity: 17 litres.

Morini were founded in 1946 by a bloke called Alfonso, making BSA Bantam type commuters for a war weary Italian nation.

❝**We didn't get it for the same reason we don't understand cheese for breakfast, hurling livestock off the top of churches and going to bed in the afternoon and not having sex**❞

Moto Morini

DR350

Suzuki

Best dual purpose bike

emember Ronco? They were the people who sold stuff – usually to do with the kitchen or personal hygiene – that was 'not available in the shops.'

Instead you had to 'send a cheque or postal order' – the typical punter being more likely to own a talking cat than a credit card. There were two things about Ronco: first, the stuff that it sold was total shite and second it always did more than one thing – corkscrews that doubled up for removing ear and nose hairs; jumper

defuzzers that, with a local anaesthetic, could be used for small operations. This brings me to the DR350 – a dual-purpose motorcycle from the eighties but not, thank Kevin, a Ronco product but rather one

from the Suzuki Motorcycle Company of Hamamatsu, Japan. With its gutsy 350cc motor pushing out around 24 hp through a six-speed gearbox allied to its light weight, the little DR had a top speed not far off

■ Should your Sunday ride include sections of the Shetland Isles, this bike is perfect for you

❝the first dual purpose on/off road bike that really worked❞

three figures and fuel consumption up around 60mpg.

If you were looking for a top value tool to get you to work and a comfortable companion for trips out at the weekends, then for three grand back in 1991 most people were of the opinion you couldn't do better. If, however, you were looking at some fairly serious off-road endeavours then the long travel suspension, instant throttle response (for a four stroke) and quick steering would have been enough for

anyone but the crustiest dirt demons, if you get my drift.

What I'm trying to say is that the DR350 was the first proper dual-purpose on/off road bike that really worked in both worlds. Except, of course, that BSA and Triumph had done the same thing for their booming US off-road market in the early 60s with almost every single cylinder four stroke they possessed.

The DR350 is (still) available in shops. It also removes stubborn clinkers without fuss or creams.

VITAL STATISTICS

Engine: 347cc single cylinder, four stroke, engine. Estimated peak power: 24bhp @ 7,250rpm. Dry weight: 143kgs. Fuel capacity: 13 litres. Estimated top speed: 95mph

The DR350 engine can also be found in the Suzuki Goose pocket sized sportster, which means it's very slow.

GPZ900R

Best big bike of the 80s

Kawasaki

In the 70s, there was the Z1900. Its successor in the eighties was every bit as mind-blowing and influential. The GPZ900R was the yardstick by which any other water cooled, transverse four cylinder sports machine had to be judged and, brother, it went like nothing else around. Good for over 150mph, if you could find a straight long enough and had balls of galvanized steel.

Like the original Honda CB750, the GPZ900 was a four cylinder superbike which became a blueprint for other manufacturers, particularly the engine.

With its side mounted camchain, it was a narrow unit – essential when adding a water cooling jacket to a four pot bike engine. Four valves per cylinder gave great top end breathing too. The whole engine

> **❝The GPZ was pokier than a hedgehog holding a sharp stick❞**

was designed to give its best at high revs, delivering a typically Kawasaki kick once you wound the throttle open.

The GPZ was pokier than a hedgehog holding a sharp stick, making an arse-twitching 115bhp at 10,500rpm, which was enough to catapult the rider from a standing start to 100mph in less than 10 seconds.

Of course all that would've been little more use than a psychiatrist in Baghdad without a chassis to handle the power, but Kawasaki had taken care of business there. The tubular steel diamond frame featured massive bracing around the crucial headstock area, to prevent the handlebars from flapping like John Inman's hands at a semaphore school.

Suspension too was state of the art, with multi-adjustable forks and Kawasaki's Uni-Trak monoshock system at the back giving an excellent ride.

Nowadays, the GPZ seems a bit vague, but if you go back and sample stuff like the

VITAL STATISTICS

Engine: 908cc DOHC, four stroke, transverse four cylinder, water cooled. Gears: six speed.
Estimated peak power: 115bhp @ 10,500rpm.
Estimated top speed: 150mph.

In 1986 Kawasaki brought out the RX1000 to replace the 900R. It flopped so badly that they ceased production 18 months later.

VF1000 Honda or FJ1100 Yamaha, you can appreciate how good the GPZ900 Ninja really was. For the first time, a big bike could be hustled through backroads with the same agility as a motorcycle half its size. Just after its launch in 1984 the GPZ900R decimated the opposition in the Production TT, which is no mean feat.

Apart from a few camchain and carb glitches on the early models, the GPZ900 proved to be every bit as bullet-proof as most other big Kawasakis and the company were still selling brand new 900 Ninjas in the mid-1990s, such was the popularity of the bike. Unlike many sports machines now, the GPZ was a long machine, built for big blokes to go blasting around the countryside on, with some real anger and fire in its soul.

In some ways, it was the last of the really mean Kawasakis... although thankfully, they had the decency not to paint it lime green.

■ **1984: 0-100 in ten seconds - still isn't bad today**

Most bizarre big Italian cruiser ■

■ Man met motorbike on the Centauro: motorbike usually won

I know what you're thinking; a V10 cylinder engine in a motorcycle – that's crazy. Well, it would be, but in reality Guzzi are still plugging their old Second World War army engine into an ever increasing variety of motorcycle chassis. The Centauro is most definitely one bizarre looking machine however, designed by a Sgnr Luciano Marabese who is reportedly renowned across all Italy as an avant garde kitchenware specialist – only a Latin nation could take a spatula so seriously...

The concept behind the bike according to Guzzi was to illustrate "Man meeting motorbike" which is perilously close to the sort of tripe Brian Sewell might utter if he clapped eyes on this motorcycle in the Tate Gallery. Ultimately, it's all a matter of taste, yet there's no denying that the flowing lines of the bodywork are almost beautiful, in a sort of brutal way. But sit on board the V10 and you're instantly aware of the width of the bike; it feels like sitting astride an upturned canoe. Like that other weirdo bike, the Bimota Mantra, the Centauro is actually very pleasant to ride and pretty conventional in its engineering. There's a one piece chrome molybdenum

spine frame, which must weigh half a ton, as it supports that immense engine unit. There's around 90bhp lurking inside those fuel injected twin cylinders, which is more than plenty for something designed to turn heads in the piazzas of Milan, not play racer at Misano. The Centauro probably tops out at 130mph or so, but anyone buying this for speed or fast cornering is obviously from another planet, with the neck muscles of a bison.

Beefy White Power upside down front forks, coupled with manhole cover sized front discs by Brembo, may tempt you into going deep into roundabouts now and

> **❝anyone buying this for speed or fast cornering is obviously from another planet, with the neck muscles of a bison❞**

again, but shifting the 205kgs of weight in any meaningful way will soon cure you of such madcap ideas. This is a cruiser, so cruise. Or crash. There's something to be said for commissioning outside design teams to come up with concept bikes, because the market is so conservative, biking needs shaking up now and again. But for every showstopper, there's an Aprilia Moto 6.5, or a Centauro – something which doesn't quite come off. The thing is that, more than any other European engine, the big, lazy, pulsing Guzzi twin is the obvious choice for a radical or Harley-esque cruiser, yet nobody can seem to house it in a truly gorgeous looking motorcycle.

VITAL STATISTICS

Engine: 992cc air cooled, transverse V-twin, four stroke, 8 valve engine. Gears: five speed. Final drive: Shaft. Dry weight: 205kgs. Wheelbase: 1475mm. Estimated peak power: 90bhp @ 8200rpm. Estimated top speed: 130mph.

The Centaur was a mythical creature, half man, half horse. There are no known descendants... except for Peter Beardsley.

Moto Guzzi

73 TRANSALP 600V

The original two-wheeled Range Rover

Rally Touring. Ever heard of it ? No, me neither. In fact it sounds chillingly close to some sort of treasure hunt organized by librarians from Swindon. But rally touring was the activity which Honda's PR machine ascribed to the Transalp 600 back in the mid-80s, which kind of detracted from what was a well thought motorcycle. Some might argue that BMW were the first bike manufacturer to produce what could be tagged a two-wheeled Range Rover, but the crude, agricultural engined R80GS was much closer to a short wheelbase Land Rover in truth. No, it took Honda – the company who love concept bikes – to make a machine which looked svelte and modern, whether it was parked outside a Soho eaterie, or a Shropshire silage pit.

Powered by a bored out version of that corporate dud, the VT500, the Transalp had around 50bhp in its bores, which was enough for top speed of 110mph, or all day cruising at 70–80mph, which was that bit more relaxed than the average big trail-bike of the era. Its long travel 41mm air assisted forks and Pro-Link monoshock rear end also added a much needed touch of civilization to the off-roader motorcycle, making the Transalp one of the great undiscovered commuter bikes of the 80s. Many people insisted on crashing through the pot-holed, tarmac-scarred city streets of London on sportbikes, crushing vertebrae as if they'd done 10 rounds with Giant Haystacks, when they could have been effortlessly wafting their way to another dull day at the office on a Transalp. Yet at one point, Honda were struggling to sell over 180 of them in an entire year. Bizarre.

True, it wasn't a cheap bike, but it reeked of quality like a Glaswegian child smells of fried Mars bars, with its excellent half fairing, durable engine bash plate, smooth power delivery, comfortable seat and mirrors which actually gave you an idea of what was going on behind your back. It also offered decent pillion accommodation, which was a bit of a novelty compared to most trailbikes. No, the Transalp had style, long distance comfort and respectable off-road ability despite its slight weight disadvantage. It's still in production today and Honda have sold over 60,000 worldwide. Yes, 60,000 Transalps – maybe you should try one, you might just like it.

VITAL STATISTICS

Engine: 583cc V-Twin, OHV, water cooled, four stroke. **Gears:** five speed. **Chassis:** Duplex cradle frame, 41mm air assisted front forks, multi adjustable monoshock with Pro-Link mounting system. **Braking:** Front 276mm disc, rear 130mm drum. **Estimated peak power:** 53bhp @ 7500rpm. **Estimated top speed:** 110mph.

If you are an idiot librarian, the Transalp has the words "Rally Touring" on its side to assist classification.

■ **Practical Classic: the only transport more sensible than a transalp is a bus pass**

"people insisted on crashing through the city streets of London on sportbikes, crushing vertebrae as if they'd done 10 rounds with Giant Haystacks, when they could have been effortlessly wafting their way to another dull day at the office on a Transalp"

FORMULA 125

72

Italjet

Best 'Fireball XL5' bike

Yes, I know, it's a scooter. But the Italjet Formula 125 is a scooter in the same way that Balmoral is a country cottage, that Harrods is a corner shop, and that a jacuzzi full of airhostesses is a bath. A machine that started out as a celebration of simplicity came to have a twin cylinder, liquid cooled motor, disc brakes, all round hub-centre steering (how mad is that exactly?) and styling so outrageously radical it can induce slavering fits in the teenage boys it's aimed at quicker than any ultra-violent Japanese animation.

In Italy the domestic market for 125cc machine is contested with a ferocity that makes the goings-on at Serie 'A' look like a kickabout in the park. The average teenager is indulged to a degree that would make the Sultan of Brunei feel hard done by and if their parents have to sell an internal organ so that little Gianni can have the latest, hottest maddest stroker on their piazza, then so be it.

I once spent a whole day scooting around central London on an Italjet F125

■ Most scooters are essentially the same thing, so choose the sexiest or the fastest. The Italjet F125 is probably both

> *the Italjet Formula 125 is a scooter in the same way that Balmoral is a country cottage, that Harrods is a corner shop, and that a jacuzzi full of airhostesses is a bath.*

and to be honest if you're an exhibitionist, and quite obviously I am, then life doesn't get much better. I found the vicious rear disc particularly useful for howling the tyre at crossings, forcing Japanese tourists to leap back on the pavement like spawning salmon and the F1 replica paint job – if you don't go for the Ferrari rosso corse you're missing the entire point – unbeatable for getting into meaningful intercourse with long-haired big-chested Italian exchange students. And they're just the blokes...

The Italjet F125 is the sultan of scooters. A titan of twist-and-go. A Prince among 'peds and you could market them as hairdryers, for girls. Only kidding scooter fans. The truth is that Vespa is

quite brilliant for many reasons, but the Italjet F125 is a Pavarotti-sized barrel of Chianti's worth of laughs.

If you're of the opinion that these 70mph baby rocketships should be out on a racetrack, then you're right, and they are. But scooters like the Italjet deserve to be seen because they are such stunning examples of modern technology and sharp Italian design. So show off baby.

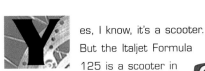

VITAL STATISTICS

Engine: 122cc two stroke, single cylinder water cooled engine.
Estimated peak power: 12bhp @ 7,500rpm.
Estimated top speed: 75mph.
Dry weight: 81kgs.
Fuel capacity: 7 litres.

Pop star Ian Brown used to ride a Vespa with the slogan 'Stormtroopers in Sta-prest' written on the side. Hmm.

Laverda

JOTA 1000

Best three cylinder Italian bike

Some motorcycles have the look of power imbued deep within their paintwork, and the Jota is one such animal. The three cylinder, 1,000cc "Beast of Breganze" was reputed to be the fastest production machine of the mid-70s at a staggering 140mph, which was a good 15mph quicker than most of the competition at the time.

Whether it was actually that fast is largely irrelevant. The Laverda was an Italian bike with German electrics and Japanese switchgear. The factory took the best from parts suppliers around the world, then assembled it on their big, brutal, ground shaking triple. This was a man's machine, built for speed, stability and high speed cornering.

The Jota was a tuned up example of Laverda's 3C model, which had been developed as a result of British Laverda importers Slater Brothers sorting out some extra horsepower for UK buyers. The factory liked it

VITAL STATISTICS

**Engine: 981cc DOHC three cylinder, four stroke, air cooled.
Gears: five speed. Estimated peak power: 90bhp @ 7,850rpm.
Estimated top speed: 130mph.**

Laverda's main business during the 1970s was making combine harvesters.

■ **Raging Bull: rarely has a bike offered such raw excitement**

> ❝the bike is so tough it could withstand a direct hit from a nuclear weapon❞

so much, it went into production – the Jota won proddie races straight from the crate.

All you need to know about this bike can be learned as soon as you fire up its high compression engine and stand well back. It is loud. That's LOUD, all right? There's a special sort of sound which emanates from triples, but the Laverda in particular has a horny, rough-edged sort of rasp to it that would put even Rod Stewart to flight.

Like many other Italian sports bikes, riding the Laverda is a sensory experience. You sit wrapped around that huge fuel tank, ears battered by the wind and exhaust noise, rear end slapped by the boneshaker-hard suspension, hands struggling to work the stiff controls. It isn't easy to get the best from such a crude – almost agricultural – motorbike, but when you do it feels great and you always remain utterly convinced that the bike is so tough it could withstand a direct hit from a nuclear weapon.

That just makes you wanna ride it, hard.

FLYING SQUIRREL 70

Best classic British two stroke

Is that an insane name or what? Wooler once made a bike called the "Flying Banana" too, but let's not get sidetracked from this innovative early two stroke hooligan machine.

Alfred Angas Scott was one of those headstrong Yorkshiremen who knew best and he rejected four stroke side valve technology in 1908 and built a light, yet surprisingly nippy, two stroke twin, set canted forwards in the duplex cradle frame downtubes. It also featured water cooled barrels and heads plus prototype telescopic forks.

After the war, old Alf lost the plot somewhat and flogged the Scott factory to go and make some outlandish sidecar project called a Sociable. So the 498cc and 596cc Flying Squirrels were the final incarnations of his early designs, but essentially unchanged. In many ways, the Squirrel sums up all that's worth knowing about two stroke technology until Ernst Degner invented the disc valve in the 50s.

What the Scott offered was an alter-native to the plodding, four stroke characteristics of most British bikes, something altogether more individual and slightly rebellious. It was a genuinely lightweight yet powerful mid-sized machine, which had a racy, raucous side to its character. You could race, hill climb or, famously, compete

VITAL STATISTICS

Engine: 498cc/596cc, twin cylinder, liquid cooled, two stroke.
Gears: two or three speed.
Estimated top speed: 75mph.

The official club magazine for Scott owners was called "Yowl."

> the Squirrel sums up all that's worth knowing about two stroke technology

in trials aboard the Scott – it was versatile.

Sadly, the Scott never really made any fundamental leaps ahead in stroker technology and it became a post-war, expensive oddity by 1946. But for diehard fans, the distinctive smoke and noise of the Scott was something to remember.

■ **Great Scott! An updated variation on Alfred Scott's 1908 original – the silk 650cc – was being sold as late as 1979**

Moto Guzzi

Best Italian touring bike

This one was no contest, despite the fact that the California has been around since Wishbone Ash were considered a daring, avant-garde rock band. It all comes down to one word when you want a motorcycle which will circle the globe – reliability.

Now I'd be the first to admit that using the word reliable in the context of anything Italian is usually proof of an unstable mind, but the California is different. You see this bike has a big, lumpy, shire horse 1100cc V-twin engine which began its working life as a 700cc Vee in the Second World War as a power unit for smallish army lorries.

It was slow then, and it's still slow now, half a century down the road. But this tractor unit just keeps on pulling baby, punting the California's slightly vague chassis forwards at a steady 70mph for as long as the world's oil supply lasts out. It may have a gearbox more suited to a Norfolk threshing machine *circa* 1890, and a braking system so weird that you'd be forgiven for thinking a Frenchman invented it, but the old Guzzi bus has its good points too.

Let's start with comfort. Not all-day-in-saddle comfort. No, I'm talking all-year-round motorcycling here, with a saddle so plush that even the laziest member of the aristocracy would feel pampered. The windscreen ahead of the rider is sensibly upright, knocking cold air, rain and splattered insect horror aside with ease.

> *practically bullet proof and weighs the same as the Heysham ferry*

Naturally, the Guzzi has fitted luggage to cart about your extra large Y-fronts or M&S Hip-Shaping Knickers (or melon gatherers as they call them in the trade, I believe) and any kitchen items you may need on your travels.

You see, the California is the exception which proves the rule. All Italians are obsessed with speed at any cost, but they are still capable of accepting that others in the world may need to trot about at the speed which cabbages grow.

So they made one bike for those people, using their oldest, heaviest, clunkiest

■ Guzzi use a patent linked braking system which has taken 25 years not to catch on...

engine. Then they kind of change the paint and the odd light switch on it every three years. Good on 'em I say, for the California 1100 is a bike which is practically bullet proof and weighs the same as the Heysham ferry, yet remains easy, relaxing and fun to ride.

VITAL STATISTICS

Engine: 1064cc transverse V-twin, four stroke, air cooled, fuel injected. Gears: Still trying to change up! Estimated peak power: 65bhp @ 6,400rpm. Estimated top speed: Canter.

Almost every Italian marque has tried an American-style machine. Most are deeply embarrassing – the Cali is brilliant in comparison.

Best big brutal hot rod

Extreme noise terror.

Those three little words sum up the essence of the V-Max experience. Like the gas guzzling-monster V8-powered American muscle cars of the 60s and 70s, Yamaha's Mad Max will take you to the edge and then go a bit faster, turning your brains into melted Pot Noodle along the way. It is the meanest, baddest sonofabitch in motorcycling.

If you do get to ride one, make sure it is the full 145bhp model, developed in one of the toughest, horniest looking V4 engines ever designed. It has the sort of torque which would make you a strong contender in a tractor pulling contest, catapulting you forwards from as little as 2,000rpm.

Although there's no fairing, the V-Max will take you to the dark side of 150mph, should you possess balls of steel and no brains to speak of. However, just remember one thing as you twist the throttle in

VITAL STATISTICS

Engine: 1198cc four stroke, vee four cylinder. Dry weight: 282kgs. Estimated peak power: 145bhp @ 8500rpm. Estimated top speed: 155mph.

The V-Max fuel tank is a dummy; the real fuel tank is located under the seat.

a Jack Nicholson Joker-type frenzy of mayhem – this bike does not go around corners, period.

The combination of kicked out front forks, Mr Softy ice cream rear shocks and a frame which is as spindly as the ribcage on Kate Moss encourage the V-Max to mis-

behave – sometimes violently – should you be rash enough to attempt serious swervery.

But that's part of the bike's psychopathic charm. Like the hot rods of Southern California, this machine was only meant to excel in a straight line, and it does that incredibly, breathtakingly well. The Yamaha V-boost fuel system seemingly pumps neat adrenaline through those awesome cylinders, making every tiny movement at the throttle an invitation to break the next speed limit. The fact that the bike looks like a refugee from the set of *Mad Max 2: The Road Warrior* is just one of life's lucky breaks.

Max Power.

Yamaha

'the meanest, baddest sonofabitch in motorcycling'

■ **Max Power: Yamaha use the V-Max motor in a snow-mobile, a jet ski and a golf buggy. (That last one's a lie)**

Best hooligan sports motorcycle

The great thing about motorcycling is that it attracts so many different types of people – we live in an age where there's a bike for everyone.

Now some people like to cruise, others want to tour the world, but there's a hard-core element in biking who just want to cut loose, maybe raise a little hell and have a few fast moments before they get too old.

If that sounds like fun, then the GSXR750 was made for you. From the day it surfaced in 1985 – an anorexic chassis housing a growling engine – this bike had the look of a mean, lean junkyard dog in its bug eyes. It was lighter than anyone thought a 750 class sportsbike could be, which in turn gave it neck-snapping acceleration and the kind of handling which immediately attracted proddie racers

of the "brain-out" persuasion.

Through the late 80s and early 90s, the GSXR750 was the standard by which other sporting 750 machines were judged. It grew heavier and occasionally handled badly – it even sported a water-cooled engine – but it never lost that bad boy reputation.

Owning a GSXR made you a bit of a lad, bringing out an aggressive, knee-down riding style in perfectly respectable librarians on Sunday mornings. Grown men with cardigans and tartan jim-jams were suddenly transformed into rabid, cackling Mr Hyde characters once they got the hang of their GSXR.

Suzuki had also made one hobnail boot of a motor in the shape of the 750cc DOHC air cooled power unit, which became one of the favourite tuning choices for a whole generation of nitrous oxide, aviation

> ### VITAL STATISTICS
> **Engine: 749cc double overhead camshaft, water cooled, 16 valve, four cylinder, four stroke. Gears: six speed. Estimated peak power: 118bhp @ 12,300rpm. Estimated top speed: 150mph.**
>
> **A race team once campaigned GSXR Suzukis and was sponsored by Durex.**

fuel, turbo charger sniffing nutters. The archetypal Streetfighter motorcycle of the early 90s – resplendent in its psychotic paint job, jacked-up rear and meaty front forks – was usually based on the GSXR750 or its bigger 1100cc brother.

Why?

Very simple really – the streetfighter cult evolved from the need for cheap speed. If bodywork was already scuffed from a minor accident, so much the better – that was going to be ripped off anyway. These bikes weren't being built by hairdressers from Camden Town called Derek. Streetfighter machines were Mad Max refugees, bristling with raw power and exhaust pipes which split eardrums at Motorhead concerts.

Even today, with hi-tech fuel injection, smooth styling and safe, sanitized handling which makes it almost novice friendly, the GSXR still has the power to make you want to just twist the throttle and go crazy. That makes it one great motorbike.

> ### " this bike had the look of a mean, lean junkyard dog in its bug eyes "

■ Headbanger's Ball: the 'Gixer' is the favourite choice of adrenaline junkies looking for a quick fix

Best rotary engined motorcycle

 ot too difficult a choice this one, as the rivals include such 70s disasters as the Van Veen and Suzuki RE5, plus a DKW with all the attractive qualities of a broken vacuum cleaner.

The Norton F1 was one of those classic British Worldbeater sagas, which, despite heroic efforts by the many, was doomed to failure by the greedy, incompetent and just plain criminal few. The rotary project languished in a shed somewhere in the Midlands for about 12 years, whilst misguided patriots kept pumping cash into prolonging the life of the Triumph Bonneville. Then suddenly, a new range of Norton rotary bikes appeared in the late 80s.

The F1, styled on the Honda CBR600 by British design house Seymour Powell, looked like something very special even before it turned a wheel. With scooped, flowing body panels, a racy riding position and some top notch components like Brembo brakes, the Norton was rated as a contender.

Despite having a budget of around £38.50 per meeting plus some fag coupons from John Player, the Norton factory went road racing with their new bike in the early 90s and, blow me down with

Hugh Grant's friend, they actually did all right. The rotor tipped Wankel design engine caused ongoing argument about the exact cubic capacity of the bike however, but most agreed it was 588cc, which put it out of the GP500 class.

For a 600 class roadbike, it was fast, kicking out 90bhp or so, catapulting the lightweight, wonderfully compact Spondon

> ❝ The rotor tipped Wankel design engine caused ongoing argument❞

chassis to around 135mph. The suspension was also sheer class, with White Power upside down forks and multi adjustable monoshock rear. But the F1 was lacking in some detail areas. The rotary engine had a tendency to "hunt" at part throttle openings, and the transmission was a botched lash-up. Plus Norton wanted almost £13,000 for it, or the cost of three CBR600s.

Oh well, back to the drawing board chaps…

■ Capacity Quandry: working out the cc of a rotary is like juggling egg-yolks…

VITAL STATISTICS

Engine: 588cc rotary; no cams, no valves, no pistons going up and down. Gears: five speed. Estimated peak power: 90bhp. Estimated top speed: 135mph.

The first rotary engined Nortons on the road were used by traffic policemen in the mid-80s.

Greatest Italian road bike ever

'a great granite-hewn sculpture of red, white and blue that oozes class'

■ Arturo Magni, the most famous MV Agusta engineer, still makes MV replicas today

Pure genius.

Yes, it's that much-used expression which captures the beauty, the power – the sheer romance – of the MV Agusta. Here's a bike straight out of a Fellini movie or a Ferrari museum. This is the Italians doing what they do best; posing.

Of course, there's more to it than that, because MV racked up more 500cc class Grands Prix wins than John Wayne did cowboy movies in the 50s and 60s, and the engineering lessons they learned in making Bell-Agusta helicopters helped keep their motorbikes pretty much on the pace. For many years, the Italian Count who ran MV Agusta refused to make a roadgoing version of the racebike, but when he did finally authorize a 750cc sized replica, what

a stunner it was...

The heart and soul of this beast sucked fuel like a dipsomaniac through four carbs into the sandcast, all alloy, double overhead camshaft, 743cc four cylinder engine. With shaft final drive like a car, the MV was a sophisticated machine by contemporary standards, as befitted something which cost at least twice as much as the average big Japanese bike.

It also handled superbly, despite its considerable weight, using the best Italian suspension components of its time grafted onto a massively braced frame.

The MV wasn't perfect. Like so many Italian machines of the 60s/70s, it suffered from poor component quality control – in truth, bits sometimes fell off it. Still, it was an accomplished ride for the well-heeled enthusiast who felt like playing at

being Agostini on Sunday afternoons.

But it is perhaps in the final analysis, the style of the thing, that the MV Agusta becomes worthy of legend. It is so, so beautiful, a great granite-hewn sculpture of red, white and blue that oozes class, Italian brio and svelte speed. Just run your fingers along the sides of its immense fuel tank, peer inside the carb bellmouths, then note the brazen stance of the four matt black exhaust pipes. This bike rocks.

In that respect, it doesn't matter too much what the MV 750S is actually like to ride. In its time, it was the NSR500 GP race winner – the bike that everyone else had to struggle to beat. The MV Agusta earned its place in the sun.

Best bike for petite girls in leather mini skirts

See your bike? It's a girl's bike that is.

Yes, the Virago may be one of the better mid-sized cruiser motorcycles ever made, with respectable handling and adequate performance, but at heart it's a bit of a softy.

There's no shame in it really. The 535cc V-twin engine isn't going to eat Harleys for breakfast and spit them out as two inch nails, but it can make nearly as much power and get the Yam up to an indicated 100mph should you require it. More usefully, it burbles along all day at 60mph like a mad old woman with a free bus pass to Skegness.

The Virago also looks nice and shiny in a cheesy kinda way, with plenty of chrome bits and a funky set of slash cut exhaust pipes. Of course, the noise which emanates from these pipes is about as threatening as Val Doonican on valium, but never mind.

A whole warehouse of two-bob gimmicks, placcy mudguard flaps, die-cast alloy cissy bars and God knows what else are available for you to tart up the Virago like a spoilt eight-year-old let loose in a pony riding school. If you have no shame, you too could look like Ivana Trump's less tasteful sister.

But on the road, it is one of the best motorcycles which anyone can start a two-wheeled

VITAL STATISTICS

Engine: 535cc, V-twin, four stroke, air cooled. Gears: five speed. Estimated peak power: 42bhp @ 7,500rpm. Estimated top speed: 105mph.

The Virago's fuel tank is always empty, because the real petrol tank is located underneath the seat.

career on. It has non-threatening power delivery, steady handling and OK braking. To cut a long story short, it does everything with smooth predictability. That makes it easy to learn the basics of biking on, plus the Virago 535 boasts one of the

lowest seat heights this side of a bandy-legged Daschund, so shorter people can feel safe on it when they have to stop at traffic lights.

Whatever you think of cruiser bikes, you should reserve judgement on the 535 Virago until you actually ride one, because in the real world not everything that glitters is gold, yet the baby Yamaha does deliver the goods for comfy, all day long cruising.

Just don't try and join an outlaw gang beyond Chelsea, will you?

❛you too could look like Ivana Trump's less tasteful sister❜

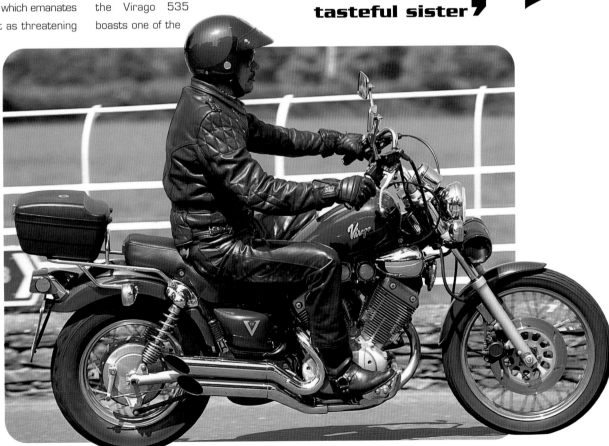

■ **Screaming Queen: if the 535 is just too much motorcycle, you can always get a 250cc...**

Piaggio

Best back to the future scooter

Blackpool, Bangkok and the past, great places to visit all of 'em, but you wouldn't want to live there, would you? Admittedly, they all offer a blend of tawdry entertainment, the chance to get hog-whimperin' drunk for pennies and dodgy sexual encounters which, to be frank, I'm as keen on as the next bloke but after a fortnight it can wear pretty thin (if you know what I mean).

The past looked great but of course it didn't work. Riding a thirty-year-old bike today is like using an outside toilet, keeping coal in the bath or taking a tablespoon full of cod liver oil every day to ward off rickets: it's unpleasant, unnecessary and fraught with danger. The only thing worse than riding a middle-aged motorcycle is finding yourself in the wobbly world of the senior citizen scooter. So Piaggio the Vespa people have decided to do a Harley-Davidson and repackage their own past for consumption by 21st century punters. The ET4 'Timesurfer' looks like it came straight out of a flashy and facile feature film about the swinging Soho scene of the sixties. Ride one and you imagine yourself as an upstart working class lad on the make just popping round to Kensington to give some posh debutante a good seeing to before heading out to a nightclub with women in leopardskin bikinis dancing in cages... Sorry, I got a bit carried away there but the period features like the pulsating metallic paint and the chrome ringed clocks are absolutely spot on. Among the less than fab and groovy features of the old-style Vespa experience were the infuriatingly awkward clutch-and-gears handshift mechanism and the irritatingly underpowered two stroke

engine. The process of refuelling took a steady hand and a strong nerve – there are mods still in counselling twenty or thirty years on after spilling Silkolene all over their white Levis . Happily both of the mediaeval practices have been disposed of and the 'surfer sports a fully automatic four stroke motor with enough guts to get you the hole shot in the traffic light grand prix.

At around 55mph the 'surfer runs out of steam, but would you want to go any faster in a open-faced helmet, wraparound Raybans and Noel Gallagher's kagoul? No,

you wouldn't. The handling is hugely improved – you won't get your knee down, but you could quite easily scuff the suede on your Clarks' desert boots.

A back to the future classic.

❛riding a thirty-year-old bike today is like using an outside toilet, keeping coal in the bath or taking a tablespoon full of cod liver oil every day to ward off rickets❜

■ Steve still has original
singles by Bad Manners

49

62 K1200RS

The most interesting brick-shaped object from Germany

BMW

BMW are famous for their boxer twin-shaped engines of course, indeed the company has used the format almost continously as its main power unit choice since 1923. But in the early 1980s, the company saw that their lurching, tractor-like twins were being seriously outclassed by the new Japanese machines and, more importantly, bikes like Honda's Gold Wing and Suzuki's shaft drive GS1000 combined class with performance – BMW's market was under attack.

So the "brick" range of four cylinder, and triple cylinder, four

VITAL STATISTICS

Engine: 1171cc In line, four cylinder, DOHC, 16 valve, water cooled. Gears: 6 speed. Carbs: None, Bosch fuel injection. Estimated peak power: 130bhp @ 8,750rpm. Estimated top speed: 145mph.

The blue and white BMW badge signifies a propeller spinning, a reference to the company's original business of building warplanes during the First World War.

'sheer, obscene, plutocratic luxury'

■ **Blitzkreig: American tuners Lufmeister make a turbo kit to push the 'big K' past 200mph!**

stroke machines were launched. They featured ugly, slab-sided engine blocks set lengthways in their chassis. One embarrassingly bizarre attempt at offering an ultimate sports touring option, the K1 model, sent them back to the drawing board.

It took until 1997 for BMW to produce its most powerful and, in many ways, its best sports-tourer, the ultra smooth, sophisticated K1200RS. With around 130bhp on tap from its DOHC, 16 valve four cylinders, the K1200 was able to propel the rider to the

far side of 140mph with ease yet maintain some kind of calm at the same time through its supple chassis and comfortable riding position.

Using the telelever front end, the K1200RS could corner with a certain aplomb – maybe not so fluently as a Fireblade, but it was designed to be a gentleman's express, kind of a two-wheeled Panzer with leather seats and air conditioning. The only weakness in the K1200's armour is its weight. At 260kgs dry, it's about 50–70 kilos heavier than most big Japanese sports machines, which shows up when you really start pushing the bike on bumpy roads. But with its adjustable screen, aerodynamic fairing, plush seating, demon brakes and quiet yet torquey engine, the big BMW is a refined way to cover your ground fast. Like so many other BMW bikes, it just invites you to pack an overnight bag, check your Amex Gold card, leave plenty of work on for your domestic staff at home, then just take off for weekend of sheer, obscene, plutocratic luxury. There's simply nothing quite like a sumptuous German vehicle which costs loads of money for irritating the vast majority of other road users, is there?

Best six cylinder bike

Honda

The 70s can be summed up in one phrase: "Excess All Areas". From glam rock and hair length to trouser width, the decade saw some crazy wild things, but none so immensely satisfiying to motorcyclists as the Honda CBX six. A two foot wide, DOHC, six pot engine that screamed at 10,000rpm like a porsche 911 Turbo acted as the outrageous centrepiece to one of the most exciting Superbikes of the time.

> **wobbling about on bumpy corners like cellulite on a Russian female shot-putter**

■ Six, Drugs and Rock 'n' Roll: A Yorkshire CBX owners' club are so obsessed with the 24-valve double-overhead-cam six that they have it tattooed on their arms

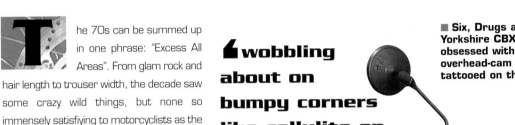

Utilizing the technology they had learned from campaigning their famous racing sixes some 10 years before, Honda created a surprisingly

docile machine for the road. The CBX's 105bhp was enough to send you to the wrong side of 130mph, but it flowed through the rev range smoother than Roger Moore drinking Guinness.

The only problem with the CBX was its sheer size. It weighed around 600lbs with fuel on board and, with fork legs thinner than a Supermodel's ribcage, feeble brakes and uninspiring rear suspension, the whole plot soon started wobbling about on bumpy corners like cellulite on a Russian female shot-putter. Not a pleasant sight.

But you have to forgive those weak spots in the overall concept and give a round of applause to Honda for having the bottle not only to do it, but to make the six cylinder opposition from Kawasaki and Benelli look decidedly dodgy by comparison. Dammit, the CBX was the only – is the only – motorcycle you can ride that shows off every inch of its six transverse engine cylinders to the world and says "Up yours mate, I'm coming through".

Scorchio.

VITAL STATISTICS

Engine: 1015cc Four stroke, six cylinder, DOHC, air cooled. Estimated average fuel consumption: 27mpg. Estimated peak power: 105bhp @ 9,500rpm. Estimated top speed: 130mph.

Launched in 1978, the CBX was one of the first bikes, along with Honda's CX500, to have tubeless tyres.

THUNDERBIRD SPORT

TRIUMPH

Cool Britannia

■ This Triumph takes the prize for being the Best Brandoesque Retro Rockers Machine

---

VITAL STATISTICS

Engine: 885cc three cylinder, four stroke, water cooled, four valves per cylinder.

Gears: Five speed.

Estimated peak power: 83bhp @ 8,5000rpm.

Estimated top speed: 120mph.

1990s Triumphs have the corporate logo embossed into the footrests.

❝It's the soul of backstreet cruising and High Street posing❞

When you have a great history, it's a shame not to recycle it. That's what makes chartbusters of the 90s like Ocean Colour Scene, Blur and Oasis considerably richer than you lot, who are all wearing flares and a tie-dyed cheesecloth shirt down at the pub on karaoke night.

John Bloor's new Triumph company goes from strength to strength as the bikes utilize the neat styling cues of the 60s Thunderbirds, Bonnies, Tigers, etc. and offer Japanese level performance and reliability in machines like the Thunderbird Sport 900. Oh and one other thing – it's as sexy as hell.

Just take a long look at this bike, from

the aggressively hunched fuel tank to the flash-harry sweep of its twin exhaust pipes. That's a little touch which pays homage to one Craig Vetter, an American stylist who worked some serious magic on the original Triumph Trident and turned it into the Vetter Hurricane, which looked madder then the Monkeemobile crossed with Batman's toybox. But still cool.

The Thunderbird Sport has power bulges and chrome knick-knacks in all the right places. It's one hunky big motorbike, something that reeks of the past yet shines like the technology of the future.

Naturally, it

goes at the sort of speeds which would have the old sixties Triumphs clattering into smouldering fragments of twisted scrap metal. The T-Bird powers forwards with the sort of low-down, dirty great lumps of torque that make the instant annihilation of dithering dolts in clapped out Datsun minicabs mandatory.

It lunges baby, packing a punch like Prince Naseem in a strop.

The 900cc engine makes for a great all round roadblaster and

it also sounds like a real motorbike should, emitting the sort of gruff, throaty sounds that turn heads when you twist the throttle in anger. The T-Bird is the Rod Stewart of biking, but before he went disco and started wearing daft scarves. It's the soul of backstreet cruising and High Street posing, yet can deliver the goods on country roads on a Sunday morning.

If they decided to re-make *The Great Escape*, then whoever took Steve McQueen's part would jump the prison camp wire on a Thunderbird Sport. Respect.

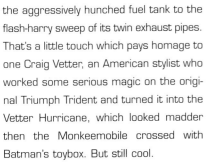

■ **The Thunderbird Sport is Triumph's sexiest new bike of the nineties**

VFR400

Honda

Best value grey bike

❝thrashed to an incredible 14,500rpm every morning❞

There are many reasons for buying what's known as a 'grey' bike, which is not some sick tribute to John Major's underpants, but a used motorcycle imported from other countries. The main benefit can be summed up in two words however; cheap speed.

But it's great to have a bit of quality too and this is where the VFR400 Honda really scores. It has a bullet proof engine which can be thrashed to an incredible 14,500rpm redline every morning as you ride to work.

The four stroke Vee shaped motor also sounds like a baby racebike, so it encourages the sort of spirited riding which brings out the best in the VFR's compact and utterly stable chassis. It's a lightweight masterpiece built around a typical late 80s twin spar frame, with a natty single sided swingarm on later VFR models.

What this translates into on the tightest of twisty backroads is sheer boy racer heaven. The tiny chassis lets you tip the VFR in ultra fast as each bend arrives with total confidence and the fact that its 59bhp

■ **Honda's RVF series race engines from the 80s spawned a generation of superb track bikes**

motor hasn't got enough horsepower to overwhelm the handling makes it highly user friendly.

Add decent brakes, a well balanced monoshock to keep your spine immune from the worst of the bumps plus a stylish, wraparound fairing, and you have the perfect roadgoing weapon for the complete humiliation of slow riders on bigger bikes.

The VFR isn't any use at touring, taking pillion passengers or having sidecars attached by men called Reginald who enjoy making scale models of English cathedrals. But it is fantastic at providing bikers with a 125mph plus frenzy of speed and sharp handling. An ideal trackday tool, which can be picked up for less than two grand.

A bargain.

MANXMAN 250

Excelsior

Best British lightweight four stroke single

nce upon a time, Britain was renowned for single cylinder motorbikes and this is one of the best, the purest, ever made. The reason comes down to simplicity, because the Manxman is all about basic engineering principles. Whether it's the 250 or 350 version, the heart of its appeal lies in that 17 jewel Swiss watch movement motor.

When you think about it, the single goes right back to the roots of bikes, because when Victorian speedfreaks were looking

> **'sums up everything you need to know about four stroke singles'**

for cheap thrills they would literally attach a single cylinder proprietary engine to a bicycle frame, thus creating a motorcycle.

From the invention of bikes to the 30s, the Manxman perhaps sums up everything you need to know about four stroke singles in one concise, elegant engine. In fact, Excelsior began business making bicycles and were the first in England to attach engines to their products and offer motorized bicycles for sale in 1896.

The Excelsior Manxman appeared in 1935 and was derived from TT-winning experience. It featured a massively strong roller bearing crankshaft, which took its drive to the top end via bevel cut gears, through a dowel pin to more gears at the camshaft. Primary drive to the gearbox was another simple arrangement of gears.

Because the Excelsior carried all its engine oil internally rather than using fiddly – and usually leaky – pipes on the side of the

VITAL STATISTICS

**Engine: 246cc/349cc four stroke, SOHC, single cylinder, air cooled.
Gears: four speed. Estimated peak power: 24bhp @ 6,000rpm (250 model).
Estimated top speed: 80mph.**

Excelsior produced an 800cc side valve single cylinder engine in 1913.

cylinder, and used an all alloy construction, it had a cleaner, more modern appearance than the typical Brit single of the era. With a cradle frame, four speed gearbox, fully enclosed valvegear and a gear drive take off point for a rev counter, the Manxman was obviously built for competition – this was the Aprilia RS250 of its day, but featuring a four stroke engine. Only the 1927 "cammy" Norton could boast anything like the same sophistication of technology, although it was a 500cc motor.

For the 30s streetracer on a budget, the Manxman 250 was the only choice.

The Excelsior Manxman was a supremely balanced lightweight machine of the times, a true racer for the road. We have to include it here because of its undoubtedly profound influence on every subsequent single cylinder engine designer looking for a blend of power, style and precision – especially one Ing. Fabio Taglioni, whose 250 and 350 racing singles achieved the same level of success in the 50s and 60s as the Excelsior Manxman had in the 30s.

■ **Fantasy Island: like the Lambretta Grand Prix, the Manxman never won the race it was named after**

TRIDENT T160 57

British bike that nearly saved the industry

Triumph

The past is another country of course and like many foreign places it is inhabited by offensively stupid people. Whatever history you care to read charting the slow suicide of our once great motorcycle industry, you cannot avoid shaking your head in disbelief at the seemingly limitless pig-headed, ignorant, incompetent and plain daft decisions of those responsible for designing, manufacturing and selling motorcycles between 1945 and 1975. It's so typically British that we always allow the greatest mediocrities in life to wield the most power, isn't it?

Sorry, I went all Ben Elton there ... where were we? Oh yeah, the Triumph Trident T160.

It started life back in 1968 as the T150 – although a 750 triple engine prototype was ready in 1963 at Triumph – which was the Triumph-badged cousin of the BSA Rocket Three, an altogether sexier machine. Both Brit bikes had their glory stolen by the CB750 Honda's appearance some six months later – suddenly a three cylinder bike didn't seem such big news.

But the Triumph/BSA backroom boys persevered with their triple, making it go ridiculously fast at the Isle of Man TT proddie races and – with the help of one brilliant frame maker, called Rob North – Triumph Tridents won some big races over in the USA, where British bike makers depended on volume sales in the 60s for their survival. Then, in 1973, BSA/Triumph went bust and for another two years, politicians, dull managers in suits, mediocre engineers and a host of other imbeciles argued over the price of brass washers and haddock, whilst the Japanese continued to sell more big bikes all around the world.

The Trident however was still a poten-

VITAL STATISTICS

Engine: 740cc OHV, three cylinder, four stroke, air cooled. Gears: five speed. Compression: 9.5:1. Carbs: Three 27mm Amal. Estimated peak power: 58bhp @ 7,250rpm. Dry weight: 525lbs. Estimated top speed: 115mph.

The last batch of Tridents made in the UK were sold to the Saudi Arabian Police.

tial best seller and, when the production lines began rolling at BSA's former factory at Small Heath, Birmingham in 1975, the revised T160V model was an altogether more blended, beautiful and smoother big bike than before. Its styling was radically improved, with clean, flowing lines, a three or four gallon fuel tank option, upswept exhausts, an engine tipped forward 15 degrees and more rakish front forks.

But Doug Hele and his team had applied some serious thought beyond the looks of the new Trident. It now had modern features like disc brakes – even if they were pretty feeble when it came to stopping a 550lb motorcycle in a hurry – an electric starter, and a new five speed gearbox,

with left side change like the big Jap bikes of the 70s.

Yet for all its faults, like a weak primary drive chain, feeble clutch and restricted ground clearance, the T160 was the best looking, most comfortable and greatest sounding big bike money could buy between 1975–77. It growled.

It also steered well and, so long as you gave it time, it handled respectably through the corners, even at speeds close to its outright maximum of around 115mph. The riding position was perfect for a whole day at 70mph. Fitting an electronic ignition cured early morning start-up blues, and the Trident accelerated with the sort of torquey lunge which an entire generation of Brit bikers were totally hooked on.

With a little more development, the Trident could have been a true flagship motorcycle for the British industry, or what was left of it, during the 1970s.

With supreme irony, Edward Turner's parallel twin engine – which had given Triumph its finest hour – was the final nail in the company's coffin.

> **'a true flagship motorcycle for the British industry, or what was left of it'**

■ **Mad in England:** *Motorcycle Sport* tested the new Trident – it wouldn't tick over, leaked oil, and was already rusty!

Honda

Beanz Meanz Dreamz

Let's get a couple of things straight right from the start shall we? It wasn't super and it was never a dream. In fact Honda's humble but honest pedestrian plodder vies with the Suzuki

■ **Worshipped by despatchers and commuters the world over**

The brilliance of a bike like this is that it demonstrates the brilliant philosophy of Sochihiro Honda better than almost any bike the company that bears his name ever built. Better than the CB750. better than the 'blade, better even than the world's best selling bike, the super Cub. Sochiro himself was a Cadillac-driving, saki-swilling wild man who only took to building bikes when he almost killed himself racing cars. But he understood that the world is full of people far more sensible than

> **❝here was a machine so utterly lacking in sex appeal that in some of Europe's catholic countries it was used as a contraceptive❞**

Freewinds, Hodaka Road Toad and a strange scooter-type contraption the Moto Guzzi Galetto, which if it had ever made it over to these shores would have been translated as the 'small cock' – the most embarrassing name ever stuck on the side of a motorcycle.

Not that most Superdream owners would actually have noticed. Since the pioneer days of belt drive and no brakes young men have become hopelessly addicted to the potent mix of sex and danger delivered by the motorcycle and countless women have been seduced by the romantic figure struck by these modern knights of the road and their steeds of steel. And yet here was a machine so utterly lacking in sex appeal that in some of Europe's catholic countries it was used as a contraceptive.

VITAL STATISTICS

249cc four stroke, three valves per cylinder parallel twin engine.
Gears; 5 speed
Dry weight; 390lbs
Estimated peak power; 28bhp @ 10,000rpm.
Estimated top speed; 90mph

A very heavily modified 250 Superdream featuring a decaying skull won the first ever Survivalist and Rat Bike Show.

himself. The sort of people who have steady jobs, steady girlfriends and ask for the usual at their local. The sort of people who go out at lunchtime and buy shirt and tie gift sets from C&A... for themselves, not their father-in-law. Instead of doing us all a favour and inventing some sort of horrific virus that could only be transmitted through wearing sandals or drinking halves of bitter he decided to build them a motorbike that reflected their comfortably numb lives, and the overweight, inconspicuous, underachieving Superdream was perfect. Here was the motorcycling equivalent of museli.

Metamorphosis

MuZ

Franz Kafka wasn't into bikes so far as we know – he was too busy trying imagine daily life as a giant insect – but he would appreciated the strange, ironic twist of history which brought about the Skorpion 660. A long time ago, when the cheery faces of Stalin, Brezhnev and their henchmen ruled Eastern Europe, motorcycles were regarded as mere transport for the fortunate few amongst the great proletariat. Factories like MZ in Germany, Jawa/CZ in Czechoslovakia and Cossack in Russia all churned out thousands of the wretched, spluttering, toxic gas-stinking two strokes, which were so dangerous to ride that most citizens preferred working nights in Chernobyl.

Then the Berlin Wall came down in 1989 and suddenly the bike factories which had enjoyed a communist system monopoly realized the game was up. No one wanted their products and one by one they slipped into terminal decline. Except MZ. There is, of course, an engineering gene within the German soul, so the works committee at Zchospau held a meeting and decided to develop their own range of new, four stroke powered motorcycles. The first of this new generation was the Skorpion 660. Initially, it was powered by a slightly agricultural Rotax engine, but a deal with Yamaha provided the 660 trail bike thumper as the basis from 1994 onwards. It's lively enough, enabling the MuZ to hit 110mph on a good day, but the bike's real selling point is its chassis, which is superb – and British designed. That's right, British designed. Seymour-Powell design consultancy in London actually won awards for their simple, lightweight twin-tubular spine frame, which carries the engine from its

> ### VITAL STATISTICS
>
> **Engine: 660cc, water cooled, single cylinder, four stroke. Gears: five speed. Ignition: electronic. Estimated peak power: 48bhp @ 6,250rpm. Dry weight; 173kgs. Estimated top speed; 110mph.**
>
> **MuZ returned to Grand Prix racing in 1998. They painted their Yamaha bike green, then realised that their green company logo had become invisible...**

elegant arches. Add sporty suspension and suddenly you have the first credible motorcycle from Eastern Europe since Ernst Degner almost won the 250 GP title in the early 1960s – which was on an MZ two stroke as it happens.

The Skorpion 660 will never be a big-selling machine, nor will it satisfy the sad, para-boot wearing army of low budget dole

> **❛Franz Kafka would have appreciated the strange, ironic twist of history which brought about the Skorpion 660❜**

scroungers who still worship at the temple of MZ two stroke technology. But it is a decent bike, from a company which metamorphosed in the late twentieth Century into a producer of real motorcycling alternatives. For that, they deserve respect.

■ **Britisher Arkitekt: Seymour-Powell penned the Skorpion's sleek lines**

MONSTER 900

Coolest retro down the coffee shop

Ducati

Some bikes look cool, others have a great name, but rarely do the two come together so perfectly. The Ducati Monster series – which kicked off with the 900cc model in 1993 – are bikes with attitude, something to be seen around town on. This is one Italian beauty which is even more monster than a top footballer's salary.

At heart, it's a simple concept; take one sluggardly Ducati 900SS engine from a pleasant enough 80s bike, tart up the trellis-type frame with the better suspension and then hand the project over to one Mr Galluzzi, who can pick stunning body-

'steers with the precision of a deadly laser in a James Bond movie'

■ **Beauty and the Beast: it looks good, it tastes good, and by golly it is good**

work designs from thin air, then re-invent the wheel after a light pasta lunch and an agreeable chianti.

There's something very special about the swoop of the Monster's seat and tail-piece unit and the delicious curve of its fuel tank which sets this bike apart from many a Japanese retro.

The trouble is that too many other bike manufacturers are so busy fretting about dealer finance incentives, computer controlled parts systems, blah, blah, blah, that they can't take a good look around at what's really going on with bikers, then make a machine that melts brains into ragu sauce.

Bikers want style, they need to look good – otherwise

VITAL STATISTICS

Engine: 904cc, V-twin, four stroke, air cooled. Gears: six speed. Estimated peak power: 70bhp @ 7,000rpm. Estimated top speed: 120mph.

This bike bears no relation to John Prescott, Jo Brand, or any other sea monster.

they'd all be pootling round on ratcatchers' MZ Simson 50s, dressed in heavily waxed pants and rubber kitchen gloves.

The Monster 900 can wheelie the entire length of your high street, it can blast away from cars in the traffic lights drag race, or you can hustle it round country roads with the best sports machines.

It not only looks heart-stopping, it features superb Brembo brakes and steers with the precision of a deadly laser in a James Bond movie. There are also two smaller 750 and 600cc sized versions of the same bike, which are ideal if you need to go slow and save money. But the 900 is the biggest, the baddest and the horniest of all the Monsters, so that makes it the one to have.

The only thing the Monster can't do is carry a passenger on the strange cooker-hob-shaped protuberance located at the back of the seat. But that's OK because, let's face it, if you are on the pull when you're out posing on your gorgeous Italian motorcycle, two's company, three's a crowd...

53 160GS

The Jesus of Cool

Scooters are different. They're sedate and really only suitable for girls and quiet newly-weds. But these pastel-coloured devices can still be dangerous. Beware of skids. Not my words but those of a Choldmondley-Warner type publication called *A Chap's Guide to The Two-Wheeled World* including other useful advice about discharging your carbine at natives while maintaining control of your Scott Super Squirrel. Out-of-print since they stopped rationing eggs. Still, doesn't mean it isn't true... Only kidding – you've got to give it to the Piaggio lads from Pontedera who've been in the engineering business since 1884. After a bit of a blow in 1945 when the Italian air force cancelled a big order for aero engines due to unforeseen circumstances i.e., losing World War Two, they decided to diversify. What they wanted was a tough, adaptable two-wheeler that would provide basic transportation for the impoverished masses. So they asked a helicopter designer... Corradino D'Ascanio knew nothing about motorcycles and that's probably why his Vespa – named for its bulbous bodywork and the distinctive buzz of its two-stroke engine – was different in every way to a motorcycle. For a start it had no frame – structural rigidity was provided by the monocoque construction of the pressed steel panels. The engine, gearbox and rear wheel all pivoted to provide rear suspension, the front forks were single sided affairs and gear changes were achieved by a left-hand clutch and shift combination. So you see scooter riders don't just have strong right wrists.

My first bike was a Vespa 50 and, as proscribed by one of the stupidest laws ever enacted by Parliament, was fitted with pedals protruding beyond the accommodating footboards making it as wide as the Major's Daimler and as slow as a lottery winner on the way to work. I hated it.

However the new Vespa ET4 is quite an improvement on the effete and under-powered output of the Pontedera works. It looks great and comes in all kinds of retro colours that won't clash with your Hush Puppies but best of all they've got rid of the ridiculous gear shift and annoy

■ **Long term love affair: Piaggio's Vespa follows a unique design**

❛it looks great and comes in all kinds of retro colours that won't clash with your Hush Puppies❜

ing two stroke engine which meant juggling with a funnel and a seeping bottle of 2T – no fun when you were wearing white Levis. Oh bugger I've given the game away, haven't I, now my secret life as a Northern Soul Boy will be splashed all over the *News of The World*.

OK,. so I've owned more than one Vespa (nine actually) – it doesn't make me a bad person, I was drinking a lot back then...

1000 EXUP 52

Best executive express for hooray hooligans

I blame sheds.

The shed occupies a pivotal position in the history of the British nation. Just think – if it wasn't for these modest wooden buildings, generations of free-thinking engineers and designers would have had nowhere to develop and exercise their imaginations and of course nowhere to hide their stash of pornography.

Today, men in sheds build specials. That is, they take apart large capacity modern (invariably Japanese) motorcycles and rebuild them with parts of other unrelated motorcycles in the bizarre belief they konw better than the employees of... say Honda, and that if you really want to make a Fireblade handle then it needs a twin shock conversion from a Hillman Imp, the front forks from a Fantic chopper and – essential this – a very, very small number plate.

The reason that people still think they can improve on the best that the mighty multi-billion dollar Japanese bike industry can muster is that not so long ago you could. The nineties and bikes like the Yamaha FZR1000 EXUP changed all that.

I still remember the very first time I rode one. Emerging from the back of a grubby Transit in pristine pearlescent white, gleaming in the glare of streetlights, I swear I salivated. I rode it right there and then. No jacket. No gloves. No helmet, no nothing. Some people will think I admit to this now in order to claim some kind of bad-boy brownie points but others will understand that I just had to ride it. The experience was of the bright-shining-light-

■ Ton-up on your EXUP: Ahead of its time

"here was the Holy Grail... I had seen God"

at-the-end-of-a-tunnel variety. Here was a big Japanese race replica that brand spanking new, straight out of the crate, felt complete. Brakes, suspension, handling, power, delivery, suspension – it felt so... together. Here was the Holy Grail – a bike with a massive 160mph stomp on the straights, but unfeasible ability in the twisties. And better than that it came without shock or surprise and allowed mere mortals to access the sort of thrillsome experience previously only available to higher beings with the reflexes of a house fly and titanium testicles. I had seen God.

The Yamaha FZR1000EXUP brought power to the people. Today its old school graphics, squared-off styling and outright obesity mean it is referred to as a sports tourer (in ten years they'll be calling it a factory custom) but this is a future classic that will never be cheaper than is now. Or you could try building something better in your shed. Just make sure you can lock the door from the inside.

VITAL STATISTICS

Engine: 998cc four cylinder, four stroke water cooled. **Estimated peak power:** 110bhp @ 10,000rpm.
Estimated top speed: 160mph.
Dry weight: 215kgs.
Fuel capacity: 18 litres.

The EXUP gets its name from the trick valve in its exhaust system which pivots to modify back pressure as you open the throttle. Just thought you'd wanna know.

Yamaha

BLACK SHADOW

Vincent

Best British V-twin ever

The Vincent.

It's a name of almost mystic proportions, and the big, Vee shaped monsters which thundered out of their Stevenage works between 1936-1950 have become possibly the most desirable of classic British bikes in modern times. The men who designed them, Phil Vincent and Phil Irving, were maverick engineers, searching for radical design solutions to push big bike performance and practicality forwards in the 30s and 40s.

The Black Shadow came along in 1948. The war interrupted development of their first V-twin, which was reputedly designed when two tracing paper drawings of their Comet 500 single overlapped on a desk. Whatever the inspiration, the Black Shadow, with its matt black engine casings, intricate pipework and girder-like chassis, oozed power and mystique like Elvis in his '68 comeback TV special.

The great lump of engine, the sort of monster Brunel would have dreamed up, was suspended from a spine frame which doubled as the oil tank. Clever stuff, but

> **❝A ton-fifty in your bathers. Crikey❞**

VITAL STATISTICS

Engine: 998cc 50 degree V-Twin, four stroke, air cooled. Gears: four speed. Estimated peak power: 65bhp.
Estimated top speed: 125mph.

In 1951 the Black Shadow cost £402 new – the same price as a terraced house in the North of England.

■ **Boy's Own Biking: the 125mph exploits of the Vincent test-riders were reported in *The Eagle* comic**

the suspension was equally advanced, with cantilevered spring damping at either end making the best of the materials at the time. A neat touch was the way the rear wheel could be fitted in either way, so that you had a choice of final drive sprockets biased for acceleration or top speed.

Ultimately, it was the statement "Fastest production motorcycle in the world" which sold the handbuilt – and alarmingly expensive – Vincent twins to discerning speedfreaks around the globe. The Shadow was good for 120mph any day of the week, and you could cash in your sugar ration books in austerity Britain by

cruising to the shops at a relaxed 90mph.

The big, brutal style of the machine matched its dark, brooding engine noise – this was a bike which boomed along. The Vincent was a motorcycle for men, not boys. Rollie Free – naked except for swimming trunks and flip-flops – lay on the fuel tank of one to clock a speed record at 150mph in 1950, at Utah salt flats.

A ton-fifty in your bathers. Crikey.

Like so much else surrounding the Vincent name, it's steeped in legend, all of which adds something to the special achievement the bike represents. In the depression of the 30s, Phil Vincent dreamed of the ultimate roadburner and, despite the costs involved, he and Irving rejected any compromise and went for it. Pure, inspired folly.

Today, bikes like the Britten, Firestorm, Suzuki TL1000, Aprilia RVS1000 and many more owe their existence to the immense grace, power and poise of the Vincent Black Shadow.

BANTAM 50

Best telegram boy bike

 magine you are a sort of Mr Cholmondley-Warner character working for the Board of Trade at the close of the Second World War. You have the choice of taking the blueprints for a farty DKW two stroke motorcycle engine or the Volkswagen Beetle car back to Blighty as the spoils of war.

No choice Mr Grayson – Britons do not wish to drive a Nazi vehicle named after a repellent insect, do they?

That was how the BSA Bantam was born in 1948, but this humble 125cc commuter motorcycle became a British icon, like red pillar boxes, warm beer and Norman Wisdom. The heart of its appeal was the basic simplicity of the German DKW design; the single cylinder 123cc alloy head two stroke featured a three speed gearbox and had few parts. It proved surprisingly reliable, so long as you added plenty of oil to the petrol for all round lubrication.

The Bantam was eventually one of the mainstays of BSA's commercial success in the 50s and 60s, exported to over 70 countries in various formats, evolving from 123, through 149cc, then ending up as a 174cc bike. An entire generation of Woodbine smoking, ration book scrawny youths grew up on Bantams, most of them hacking about on G.P.O. red 125 models, delivering telegrams to women wearing floral housecoats and too much Brylcreem.

■ **Small but perfectly formed: the Bantam was everything best about the British bike industry, i.e. it was German**

VITAL STATISTICS

Engine: 123cc two stroke, single cylinder. Gears: three speed. Fuel capacity: 1.65 gallons. Estimated peak power: 4bhp @ 5,000rpm. Estimated top speed: 55mph.

Mad as it seems, later 175cc models had their own race series and were capable of topping 90mph.

❝A British icon, like red pillar boxes, warm beer and Norman Wisdom❞

The Bantam wasn't perfect by any means. It seized easily, and flat out speed attempts caused its contact breaker points to move, or made the exhaust vibrate loose from the cast iron cylinder head. It also boasted feeble brakes, a slippery clutch and an electrical system designed for exclusive use in the sort of cars clowns drive in the circus.

But it was still so much more durable than any other British lightweight motorcycle ever manufactured – with the possible exception of the Triumph Tiger Cub – that thousands of Bantams are still around today. For many people, the Bantam was an introduction to bikes, work, maintenance skills, coffee bars and stocking-clad girls with skirts that flared up when they jived.

All that makes it the classic first British bike.

Buell

LIGHTNING S1

Best sporting American

Once you mention the word sporting, it's best to forget about Harleys unless you fancy sliding sideways on an XR750 somewhere in a part of the USA sunbelt where men called Wilbur are not ashamed to walk around their neighbourhood with a pet pig.

Erik Buell, however, has a different idea of what a sports motorcycle should be. He still loves V-twin shaped engines, which is very all-American of him, but he has the good sense to extract a healthy wedge of power from the old H-D 1200cc unit.

> **"the equivalent of two-wheeled homebrew. In the south, they call it White Lightning"**

Around 90bhp in fact, which is more than enough to stand the Buell on its rear wheel, should you feel a strange compulsion to wave your stetson and shout "Yee-Har."

That's fine and dandy, but there's more to the Lightning. For a start, it actually handles like a modern bike, which is unusual for anything two wheeled and made in the USA for lardy-assed, leather chaps-wearing, 35 stone cruiser riders called Bubba. In short, the Buell is agile, with a spindly tubular chassis, neat three spoke wheels, upside down forks and a box section swingarm. There's also a trick underslung monoshock, set beneath the engine to keep the bike nice and short. It's no Fireblade beater, but you can hustle.

Once you see a Buell, you will never mis-

VITAL STATISTICS

Engine: 1203cc, V-twin, air cooled, four stroke. Gears: five speed. Estimated peak power: 91bhp @ 5,800rpm. Estimated top speed: 130mph.

Erik Buell invented this bike by racing one – balls of steel or what?

take it for anything else. Its odd, angular shape, complete with an airbox the size of a briefcase and an exhaust straight from a plumbing supplies trade counter, gives the Lightning a motley profile. It's an acquired taste, but undeniably sets the Buell apart from the samey Japanese sporting motorcycles.

What is handy is that the Buell is just plain old fun to thrash about on. Its engine gives a good kick in the seat of your pants from anywhere above tickover, the thing goes where you point it and the brakes work well too. Hallelujah boy – it's only taken the Yanks 90 years of motorcycle development to get round to manufacturing a roadbike that can actually accomplish these basic tasks.

It might shake, rattle and roll a touch, but the Buell has got a bit of a badass heart, which to me makes it a good bike. Character, especially when it's rough and ready, is something too many motorcycle designers forget about these days, so it's OK with me if Buell want to make the equivalent of two-wheeled homebrew. In the south, they call it White Lightning.

■ **Hog Wild: the Buell's soup-plate sized front disc is the biggest in biking**

Funkiest moped

A particularly stupid piece of government legislation in the 70s allowed 50cc mopeds to develop as much horsepower as they liked, so long as pedals were fitted which could be used to ride the thing like a bicycle – just in case the owner was a twisted masochist who enjoyed using a petrol-engined vehicle like a pushbike.

The result was a small explosion in sports mopeds, the best of which was arguably the Yamaha FS1E. The 'Fizzy' as it affectionately became known, was the ultimate 'Sixteener Special' for lads in flares who all wanted to take Cherry from Pan's People down the youth club disco.

The reason was simple; power. The Fizzy was the first moped which could honestly crack 50mph without resorting to riding head first down the Matterhorn. In fact, with a bit of judicious cylinder head and porting work, a typically malnourished Deep Purple fan could expect to see a genuine 60mph on the clock, which wasn't far behind the top speed of contemporary 125cc bikes.

VITAL STATISTICS

Engine: 49cc single cylinder, two stroke, air cooled.
Estimated peak power:
6 bhp @ 8,000rpm.
Estimated top speed: 55mph.

Top British road racing hero Jamie Whitham owns a purple FS1E.

The FS1E also looked like no other moped before. Instead of being designed for penny pinching misers to go shopping for cheaper luncheon meat, the Fizzy had no baskets, carriers or similar accessories. In a nutshell, the FS1E looked like a scaled down motorbike, not a bicycle with a feeble lawnmower engine bolted onto it – a big difference.

With a dual seat, the Fizzy was tailor-made for getting your teenage kicks every summer weekend. You might not be able to go very fast, but suddenly, at the age of sixteen, you had your own cool-looking transport and were legally old enough to have sex, should you encounter a girl who was not immediately repulsed by your facial tics, zits, bumfluff moustache and overall smell of Brut 33.

For the young generation, the Fizzy was a ticket to ride.

> **❝the Fizzy was tailor-made for getting your teenage kicks every summer weekend❞**

Yamaha

■ **Gee Fiz: the classic 'Sixteener Special;' Pass me that Woodpecker cider...**

Ducati

Sexiest bike of the 70s

Dr Fabio Taglioni was a genius. Why? Because he was an engineer with the soul of a poet. What Taglioni created in the shape of his desmodromic valve V-twin in the early 70s was an engine which provided effortless, low-down power. Then, he housed that masterpiece in an endurance racing spec chassis.

Beginning life as the 750cc "round

> **❝Taglioni was the guru who gave Ducati an identity which sustains them even to this day❞**

case" Imola replica, the Ducati 900SS was a more developed version of Taglioni's rough diamond. With an achingly beautiful, slender frame, spartan seating, ultra long petrol tank and greyhound sleek half fairing, the Duke was pure streetracer. Nobody who ever heard the big Ducati snarl through open Conti silencers could doubt that.

The heart of the Ducati 900SS was the L shaped V-twin engine, however, which was devoid of camchains or valve springs. Taglioni's unique system was to fit rocker arms which opened and closed the valves precisely, whilst a bevel-cut gear arrangement connected the top end to the crankshaft. Given plenty of TLC, it worked well – if you neglected maintenance, it all went horribly wrong.

Other aspects of the 900SS were less than perfect too, including the transmis-

VITAL STATISTICS

Engine: 864cc V-twin, four stroke, air cooled. Gears: six speed. Estimated peak power: 68bhp @ 7,000rpm. Estimated top speed: 125mph.

After a long retirement, Mike Hailwood came back to race at the Isle of Man TT in 1978 on a Ducati 900.

sion and electrical system. Yet for all its Italian failings, the 900SS remains one of the most potent motorcycles of its time, not only for its 125mph speed, razor sharp handling and race victories against the odds, but also for the sheer visceral appeal of its character.

All that noise, speed and precision encapsulated in one machine summed up the Latin passion for the two-wheeled trip, and Taglioni was the guru who gave Ducati an identity which sustains them even to this day.

The desmo is dead, long live the V-twin.

■ **True Class: some bikes have a timeless beauty, an architecture of power**

The kinky Austrian aristo

KTM

VITAL STATISTICS

Engine: 609cc, water cooled, single cylinder, four stroke. Gears: five speed. Carburettor: 40mm Dell Orto. Dry weight: 149kgs. Estimated peak power: 60bhp @ 7,000rpm. Estimated top speed; 115mph.

KTM plan to stick two of these engines together to make a 1,000cc V-Twin.

Trail bikes are absolutely marvellous. There's something about blatting over hills, through streams and all that great outdoors stuff which makes me go all primordial and escapist. It all boils down to adventure I guess, the sort of instinctive curiosity to see what lies over the next hill which drove our ancestors to go and pillage an empire for themselves. The KTM company in Austria share this outward bound tendency and they make excellent trail machines. But big funky singles are good for town riding too, so in 1996 KTM produced their interpretation of the urban hooligan tool; the KTM Duke.

In essence, it's just the LC4 off-roader with a droop snoot nose fairing, dinky polished wheels and sexy upside down forks grafted on, but the sum of the parts equals much more fun that you'd expect. Why? Well the KTM Duke is like that canny old German politician, Count Bismarck – an iron fist inside a velvet glove. Start it up and the engine plods away quietly, climb on top of the bike –

using a step-ladder if necessary – then move away into traffic. You don't like traffic? No problem, just whack the throttle open in any of the first three gears and the Duke will scythe past, with its front wheel reaching for the sky, in a fraction of a second. Suddenly, you're grinning insanely.

It also steers precisely, flicks through roundabouts with aplomb and stands right on its nose when you apply the front brake. The Duke is a single cylinder, Supermotard Streetfighter, but tailored in Savile Row clothes. The White Power suspension, delicately spoked and polished 17-inch alloy wheels, the stainless steel exhaust system – it's all top class kit. Yet the KTM Duke is a motorcycle which demands

misbehaviour wherever possible. It is simply too damned good at being bad. The cost of all this quality is a trifle alarming however, which puts the Duke into the sort of territory where 750cc sportbikes are attainable. That means few people will ever get to ride a Duke in anger, and they'll regard it as some sort of weird, kinky old trailbike for rich bastards. Which it is of course, but they'll never know what fun they're missing...

> ❝ **The Duke is a single cylinder, Supermotard Streetfighter, but tailored in Savile Row clothes** ❞

■ **Kraftfahzeuge, Trankenpolz & Mattighofen... no wonder they settled on KTM**

GOLD STAR DBD34

The classic British single

If you venture down to darkest Surrey today, just past Tesco, you can still gaze in awe at the incredible, steeply banked remains of the pre-Second World War Brooklands race circuit. Stand still for a second and try to imagine thrashing the living daylights out of some clattering, teeth-loosening, oily-engined boneshaker, averaging 100mph for an entire race. Then picture yourself wearing a velvet-trimmed flying hat, goggles and riding boots for protection in the event of a "spill."

Don't fancy it, do you?

But in 1937 a man called Wal Handley, possessed with the sort of steely bravery which made respectable ladies get the vapours outside fairground boxing booths, did exactly that on a BSA four stroke single machine and was awarded – in a moment of pure *Blue Peter* type Britishness – a Gold Star.

That's like flying to the moon today in a rocket powered beer barrel, dressed only in bacofoil and a goldfish bowl, then getting a telegram saying "Well done" from the Queen.

From 1948 to 1962, the 500cc alloy engined Gold Star, manufactured to celebrate Handley's achievement, was a byword for stripped down, tall geared, thumpingly good clubman's motorbiking.

In truth, it only had about 5bhp extra over a stock 500 Beeza single, but like so many classics it had a certain mystique which set it – and therefore its rider – apart from the herd. You needed skill – and a strong right leg – just to start the thing. Then you had to be a bit special on the old twisty stuff to get the best out of the bike. Take it by the scruff and play hard.

Big singles were men's machines; single minded, loud and proud. The legend was that a good Goldie could go from 20mph to 120mph in top gear, such was its flexibility. Even if it wasn't strictly true, it was the sort of story which made the bike so much more desirable than the usual plodding, poorly assembled, dog-slow and pig-ugly British singles.

Since the Gold Star died in the mid 50s, there have been countless attempts to bring back the sort of rough, tough big biking experience it delivered. But

none have succeeded.

Why?

Well, it's like having all your Elvis Presley albums stolen and someone giving you a compilation by Shakin' Stevens as consolation, isn't it?

VITAL STATISTICS

Engine: 499cc four stroke, single cylinder, air cooled.
Gears: four speed. **Estimated peak power:** 40bhp @ 7,000rpm.
Estimated top speed: 110mph.

The Goldie was available in road racing, trials, or scrambling trim – some keen chaps would compete in all three events on the same bike.

'stripped down, tall geared, thumpingly good clubman's motorbiking'

■ Medallion Man: In parts of Northern England, being able to kickstart a Goldie was a rite of passage

44 RC45

Honda

Ultimate racer for the road

We live in a golden age of motorcycles now, with an incredible range of bikes available to anyone who wants to just go out and play on these fantastic toys every week-end.

But suppose you got a bit tasty at the old fast cornering lark. Bit of a wide boy, flash geezer, do-me-a-favour Bazza Sheene sorta thing? If you wanted one bike for scaring the hell out of yourself and all comers in any sort of road racing you cared to tackle, then the RC45 is possibly the most intelligent choice you could make.

Sure a two stroke banzai machine like Mick Doohan's GP bike is faster, but the four stroke RC45 will allow you to race, and learn, whilst keeping you on the track most of the time. It's squat, droning V-four cylinder 750cc engine produces huge gobs of poke, but with typically Honda smoothness in the mid-range. In short, you can use the force, not fear it.

The RC45 also has a chassis of such sublime ability that even novices look ultra cool on the bike. It has aplomb, a suave, Simon Templar kind of way about its behaviour at speed that lets riders get away with all sorts, then live to race another day.

Naturally the RC45 has brakes which can flatten your eyeballs, top notch suspension and a twin beam alloy frame, with

> **a high speed, fuel injected, full-on assault vehicle for twisty tarmac**

single sided swinging arm. When the world's biggest motorcycle company decide to ace their own sensational RC30 proddie bike, only the best will do. You don't tour on an RC45, or pop down the cakeshop. It is a high speed, fuel injected, full-on assault vehicle for twisty tarmac – it lives for the chase, the overtaking, the sheer thrill of clinically applied power.

VITAL STATISTICS

Engine: 749cc, water cooled, V-four cylinder, four stroke. Gears: six speed. Estimated peak power: 118bhp @ 12,000rpm. Estimated top speed: 160mph.

When the RC45 was launched it cost £18,000 – or exactly the same price as two Fireblades.

■ **Sexy single-sided swingarm was developed for endurance racing where quick wheelchanging is handy**

This is as close to a handbuilt motorcycle as Japan will come to in the cost-conscious 90s. A sensual symphony of speed, designed to reproduce the same wondrous experience every time you twist the throttle. For some people, that might seem a little soulless, too efficient by far.

But for others, the RC45 is something close to perfection on two wheels, because it is truly a machine for the modern age. There aren't many bikes which can make the rider feel surrounded by a sense of uncanny calm, of poise, at speeds above 130mph – but if you talk to anyone who has ridden the RC45, they'll tell you that's how it felt.

This is a bullet train into the twenty first century.

Best travelling brick house

Yes, I know I've said this before, but BMW do make exceedingly good touring motorcycles, mainly because their attempts at sportbikes are about as convincing as a genuinely great German rock group. Please don't mention the Scorpions or Michael Schenker, or I will have to flay you alive with old James Last albums.

The K1100LT is, however, one of motorcycling's all time great bikes. Why? Simple really – it fulfills its purpose in life. It tours, full stop. If only other motorcycle manufacturers would apply the same chilling logic, then we'd all be riding perfect examples of sporting, cruising, retro, or any other type of bike.

For a kick off, it comes equipped with waterproof, detatchable, hard panniers. So when you get to where you're going, they come off and become easy-to-carry suitcases. Excellent idea. Then you have a topbox as standard too, which is admittedly a bit on the small side, but it's something else you won't have to buy as an accessory at a later date then struggle to fit properly, using instructions translated badly from the original Mongolian. Up front, there's a superb fairing, which deflects inclement weather with the efficiency of John Prescott's trendiest suit. It also houses useful things like a clock, map pocket and a radio-cassette, for those dull, but necessary, motorway miles.

On top of all this, the K1100LT also handles bends with real aplomb, carving a steady, pre-

VITAL STATISTICS

Engine: 1092cc water cooled, transverse, DOHC, four cylinder, four stroke. **Carbs:** none – it has Bosch Motronic fuel injection. **Gears:** five speed. **Final drive:** shaft. **Brakes:** triple disc, with ABS. **Estimated peak power:** 100bhp @ 7750rpm. **Estimated top speed:** 140mph.

There is a special low seat option available which means that even someone with a 29-inch inside leg can touch the floor at junctions.

dictable line through corners no matter how rough the surface. It doesn't have a great deal of ground clearance, because it ain't a sportster, but it is capable of decking bits of its bodywork on a wet road in perfect safety – which feels amazing. This bike is safe as houses in any road situation. When you think about

it, that's one of the most important qualities any touring machine can possess, because, by definition, you are going to be exploring new places, new roads, as you tour. So when you inevitably get caught out … you won't fall off. That's especially handy in nations where the words "hospital treatment" and "unexplained death" go together like "police" and "corruption".

The K1100LT has few tiny faults, mainly down to its characterless car-type four cylinder engine, plus a pillion backrest which is so hard that sudden acceleration could turn your passenger into an invertebrate species. But, on balance, you have to respect the big "brick" as one of the best around-the-world options in biking. It's fast enough, it has a 200 mile tank range, it seats two large adults and has room for more clean pants than your mum could ever pack. One serious motorcycle.

❝it fulfills its purpose in life. It tours, full stop❞

■ 'Tomorrow, ze Vorld!' The 'big brick' was built to make trans-continental touring enjoyable

Kawasaki

Best impersonation of a cruise missile

War is a terrible business, but there's something chillingly fascinating about the toys of destruction. One terrifying example of this is the cruise missile, especially in the modern era, when TV viewers can watch a laser guided weapon hurtling low across city streets, make a left turn, then rain havoc upon one particular building with pinpoint accuracy.

The Kawasaki ZZR1100 is another kind of missile, not so deadly, but equally adept at giving the rider the eerie feeling that they are somehow one step above the road – almost flying, such is the sheer, ballistic speed of the thing. When this motorcycle appeared in 1990, it re-established Kawasaki as a maker of fast – seriously fast – performance bikes. Suddenly, the 150mph big bike had been eclipsed by a 170mph tarmac-crushing monster.

Like a low, swoopy imitation of the shark from "Jaws", the ZZR doesn't so much move as prowl. In its deep burgundy, two-tone green or pure black it looks conservative, sort of slab-sided – nothing special. But don't be deceived just because this bike doesn't boast a paint job straight from the pages of *Max Baseball Cap* magazine.

Very quietly, and very deceptively, this 1100cc, 147bhp starship cruiser can stretch your arms from their sockets just by rolling the throttle open in top gear, from as little as 40mph. It is the Lear jet of

> **❝the 150mph big bike had been eclipsed by a 170mph tarmac-crushing monster❞**

VITAL STATISTICS

Engine: 1052cc, four stroke, four cylinder, water cooled. Gears: six speed. Estimated peak power: 147bhp @ 9,500rpm. Estimated top speed: 175mph.

Some ZZR1100s were power restricted in the UK market, but you can immediately obtain full welly by fitting the carb tops with the ZXR750 model.

bikes, using its clever aerodynamic shape to slice through the air with cool, understated grace.

Admittedly, its lengthy wheelbase, slow steering and slightly overweight chassis give it a disadvantage when it comes to the corners, but it is still more than capable. There's also plenty of room for a hyperventilating pillion passenger, decent weather protection from the fairing and space to fit luggage. You can now go touring at 150mph.

OK officer, that was a joke, not an incitement to riot, but the fact remains that the Kawasaki ZZR1100 is a supremely accomplished machine at high speed. It is perhaps one of the few bikes which could race a French train from Paris to Nice yet still leave the rider wanting to carry on. Everything that makes today's motorbikes so impressive, so endlessly addictive, is here in the ZZR1100. Let's cruise.

■ **Blown Away: top USA turbo bloke Terry Kizer coaxed 460bhp from a street-legal ZZR1100**

Top British big twin

Norton

■ British beef; the Norton Commando had loads of lowdown power

Big British twins in the 60s and 70s were ridden by those blokes who believed that Old Spice was the "mark of a man". Blokes who always wore Lewis leather jackets, steel capped boots and gauntlets – even in bed.

The Commando was a sporty, fast, proper old motorbike. The sort of machine which Rockers aspired to own, even if most of them were married and driving a Vauxhall Viva when the Commando enjoyed its heyday. In moody black or deep scarlet, the 750 Norton turned heads and won instant respect on the street. It was tough stuff.

But that wasn't surprising, as the Commando had evolved from the 650SS Dominator, which was a bit of a lairy beast itself. The new 750 which appeared in 1967 was powered by a similar, parallel twin, four stroke engine, but the new feature was the updated "featherbed" Norton

> ❛the last of a majestic line of throbbing dinosaurs❜

chassis, which now mounted the vibration-prone engine in a set of rubber polo mints dotted around the frame. This dodge was given a suitably boffin-like name – the iso-lastic frame – but it did work... almost.

Later versions of the Commando grew to 850cc and were altogether more hand-some, albeit a shade slower and less funky to ride. Yet the fundamental appeal of the Norton remained tied to its big, beefy twin cylinder roots. It went fast, it handled flu-ently and – for a British bike – it was pretty reliable too. It was the first Brit Superbike and perhaps if Honda hadn't stolen its thun-der two years later with the astonishingly

smooth CB750 four, the Commando might have saved Norton.

The big Norton was the last of a majes-tic line of throbbing dinosaurs, a series of brawny, barnstorming bikes aimed fair and square at the "ton-up" merchants who liked the danger of speed and hard cornering. Men who understood power and knew how to use it. Unapproachable.

VITAL STATISTICS

Engine: 745cc, OHV parallel twin, **Estimated peak power:** 58bhp @ 6,800rpm.
Estimated top speed: 115mph.

You can still buy a brand new Commando today – they're hand-built in Staffordshire, England.

T595 DAYTONA

Best ever British bike

You might argue that classics like the Vincent, Norton Commando and the Bonneville are greater, but this is the best British motorcycle ever made because you can go out, right now, and ride this beautiful, soulful-sounding three cylinder superbike just as fast as a Fireblade. At last Britain has a motorcycle industry to be proud of and the T595 is its finest achievement to date.

The new Daytona uses the best engine Triumph have manufactured under the control of 90s factory boss John Bloor – the wonderfully grunty four stroke triple. This version is the biggest and fastest yet, churning out almost 130bhp, which is

■ Simply the best. You can take your T595 anywhere

more than enough to melt your eyeballs should you whack the throttle wide open through every gear until you reach the dark side of 160mph.

That's right, I mention the awesome speed of 160mph in the context of riding a British production motorcycle. When I grew up laughing at oil spluttering, electrically bodged, wooden-handling British bikes long ago, the very idea that anything made in this country could accomplish such a speed without resorting to high explosives seemed insane.

But John Bloor and his team have created something special here. From the tip of its metallic banana yellow headlights, through its modern art sculpture frame, to the arrogant flip of its exhaust, the T595 looks the business. Triumph went to Lotus to help get the best from its engine, they turned to Showa for suspension, and to Nissan for brakes. Like George Brough, John Bloor has learned the value of buying in the very best where it counts.

What the Triumph offers is possibly the most complete all round sporting motorcycle experience. A stunning blend of fuel-injected speed, crisp, fluent handling and reasonable levels of rider comfort. Like other big bikes

these days, it takes real skill to get the best out of it, but the rewards are totally unique.

Imagine Japanese levels of reliability, BMW quality finishing, fused together with an almost Italian passion for the sheer exhilaration of outrageous speed and style.

Daytona peach.

'the sheer exhilaration of outrageous speed and style'

■ The T595 Daytona combines craftsmanship with 90s off-the-shelf performance. It's also the sexiest Brit bike ever made

Brough

SUPERIOR SS100

Best roaring 20s bike

Known through the world as the most expensive British motorcycle you could buy, the 996cc JAP (that's J.A. Prestwich, engine builders of London, not Mr Honda's Dad) Vee twin powered speed machine was constructed to Rolls Royce standards of engineering.

George Brough was a perfectionist who insisted his motorcycles had the very best components from around the world. He personally guaranteed that the SS100 could clock the magic ton – in writing.

Each bike was the Bimota of its day; a craftsman's machine, uniquely specified to the wishes – and wallet size – of the customer. Lawrence of Arabia – otherwise known as aircraftsman Shaw in the 30s – reputedly owned eight Superiors, and, so the story goes, he ended up dying on one after swerving to avoid some children.

Brough produced other bikes, including their own radical V four, water cooled "Golden Dream" in the late 30s, but the company was always associated with this stunning machine, and what a beauty it was.

The engine featured overhead rather than conventional sidevalve arrangements, and it was the first bike in the 20s to sport a rounded, rather than "flat", fuel tank – a distinctive, silver-coloured signature. Castle forks, developed to absorb some of the shocks a rigid frame delivered to the rider, were fitted and the low handlebars, minimal luggage and pillion carrying capacity all shouted out that this was a motorcycle built for speed.

The inter-war period was an era when people were thrilled by the quest for speed. It was the time of the Schneider air trophy, the ocean liner races across the Atlantic, Bentleys and Bugattis at Brooklands. The Brough Superior's sleek, almost art deco lines, echoed that culture, celebrating the spirit of an age which dreamt that it had finished with war forever.

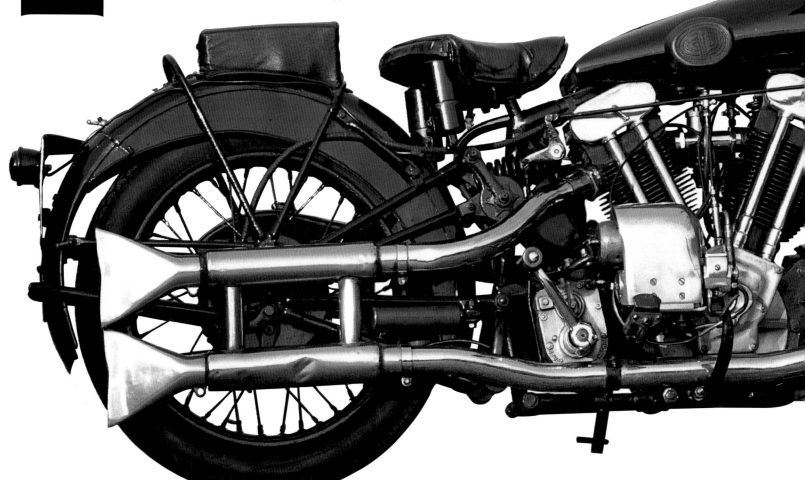

❝The spirit of an age which dreamt it had finished with war forever❞

■ "The Rolls-Royce of the Motorcycle World" – the car makers threatened to sue, but gave their permission after they visited the Brough Superior factory and found staff wearing white gloves!

GW 2275

Brough Superior

"SS 80" Model

Brough Superior

Brough Superior

Honda

The bike that shook the world

Place: The Brighton Motorcycle Show

Time: Winter, 1969.

Visitor from another galaxy: The Honda CB750.

It's difficult to imagine now, in a time when four cylinder bikes are the norm, how earth shattering the Honda CB750 must have been. For decades the British bike companies had been unchallenged in the over-500cc class, but now Honda had thrown down the gauntlet and announced to the world that the era of the Superbike was here.

The bike wasn't original in having four cylinders of course – FN, Henderson and Vauxhall had tried fours decades before, but mounted transversely, the overhead camshaft, 67bhp 750cc engine was a marvel of smoothness and meaty power. More than that, the entire bike was a well thought out package, with a front disc brake, decent handling, comfortable riding position and a sporty four-into-four exhaust system.

In its distinctive metalflake gold paint job, the Honda CB750 looked like a motorcycle from a Bond movie and sounded like a jet when you wound the throttle wide open. Flat on the tank, it could touch 120mph, but more importantly, it didn't

> **the Honda CB750 looked like a motorcycle from a Bond movie**

■ Honda Style: It may look like a Tonka toy, but the R1100GS is definitely a rider's bike, but the R1100GS is definitely a rider's bike.

VITAL STATISTICS

**Engine: 736cc SOHC, four stroke, four cylinder, air cooled.
Gears: 5 speed. Estimated peak power: 67bhp @ 8,000rpm.
Estimated top speed: 120mph.**

Honda produced a variant on the CB750 especially for lazy Americans which featured an automatic gearbox.

shake itself to bits at that speed, or spew oil all over the rider's boots like so many British roadburners of the time.

The Honda CB750 was merely the first shot in the Superbike war, with Honda bringing a range of four cylinder bikes in 350, 400, 500, 550 and 650 sizes throughout the 70s. Eventually, Honda sold a million 750 fours. Kawasaki and Suzuki soon joined the multi cylinder party and by the mid seventies, the British bike

industry was effectively bankrupt.

But the CB750 did more than deliver the final blow to Norton, Triumph and BSA. The new multi-cylinder machines triggered a renewed interest in performance motorcycles worldwide, dragging the industry out of its backstreet sheds and bringing the same sophisticated performance that a Ferrari or Porsche offered at a fraction of the cost. The man riding a CB750 could have been anybody, from a heavy metal greaser to a chartered accountant.

Honda had built the first big bike for Everyman and the world was suddenly a smaller, faster, more exciting place.

The angry Italian

All motorcycles have distinct characters – some are placid, as easy going as a Harley cruising the Florida Keys. Others are clinical, cold as a German sex therapist in a green trouser suit. However, there are few modern motorcycles which are truly angry, so full of road rage that their radiators foam at the cap like Victor Meldrew drinking fairy liquid.

The Bimota SB6R spits blood, fire and volcanic ash. This motorcycle is the dark side of mental, so hang on tight for the ultimate spine-jarring, speed-fuelled trip to 160mph.

The SB6R is perhaps the most complete, the most savage exposition of the small Italian factory's philosophy on road bikes. They take one of the most powerful engines of the early 1990s – in the shape of Suzuki's GSXR1100 – graft it inside their own exquisite, lightweight chassis, then tweak it for a bit more power.

After all, too much is never enough, right?

Now if you house a 150bhp motor in the most beautiful twin spar alloy frame you can imagine and delicately attach a few necessary items like lights, a seat, wheels, that sort of thing, the end result is well capable of making grown men ask repeatedly for their mummies.

Finally, this fabulous creation is topped off with a sinewy, aggressive-look-

■ Suits you, Sir: Bimota have been building bespoke motorbikes since 1976

VITAL STATISTICS

Engine: 1074cc four cylinder, 16 valve, water cooled, four stroke. Gears: six speed. Estimated peak power: 149bhp @ 10,000rpm. Estimated top speed: 165mph.

The aluminium three-spoked wheels are made by Antera.

ing fairing, which gives the bike the appearance of an Armani-suited bouncer standing in the dock before the local magistrates.

It's as if the bike is saying, "Look, I know I keep laughing at police cars, and that incident last week when I stamped all over the faces of those people doing a mere 120mph was out of order, but I want to change... honest guv."

Naturally, there isn't a cat in hell's chance of that, because it is in the SB6R's nature to rip up speed limits and disappear down the road like a cartoon Tasmanian Devil. Everything is geared to making the rider open

it up. The bike refuses to run slowly, spluttering at low revs, slipping its clutch if there's too much pussyfooting in town.

It needs speed; it has to just GO.

With outstanding brakes, uncanny stability beyond 130mph and a riding position which forces the pilot to get in deep behind the screen and concentrate 110% on the scary business of keeping on the road, the SB6R is a road razor, a finely oiled Purdey, a Tornado GR3 low-level attack aircraft.

Bimota have constructed the finest double act in motorcycling – a twin spar framed sculpture married to the ultimate boot boy engine. Style meets strength.

❝gives the bike the appearance of an Armani-suited bouncer❞

Bimota

36 F6C VALKYRIE 1500

Honda

Best big cruiser

Size matters.

Don't let anyone tell you different. If you want proof, just ease yourself into the saddle of this monster 1.5 litre, six cylinder engined cruiser and crush all dissenters like the worms they are.

The Valkyrie is huge; an ocean liner on two wheels, a gigantic chrome-plated iron horse for urban cowboys on speed. Its Gold Wing-based six cylinder engine gets a tune-up and a set of six into six exhausts, which exhale jet turbine-like power, and give it the snarl of a Porsche 911 Turbo. It rocks, baby, and women will worship you as a sex god just because you can hold it upright.

The astonishing thing about the Valkyrie is that the bike is so accomplished, so adept at everyday

riding. It's wheelbase is probably about the same as a Transit van, but it corners with a steady, stable predictability which lets you play silly buggers on roundabouts if you're in the mood. The brakes are outstanding considering they're stopping the motor-cycling equivalent of an oil tanker, and once you fit the optional wind-

> **'a gigantic chrome-plated iron horse for urban cowboys on speed'**

■ **It's big and it's bad: The Valkyrie weighs as much as five Italian scooters put together. And it probably takes up five times as many parking spaces too**

screen, you can easily cruise along on an autobahn all day at 120mph.

So what you get with the Valkyrie is an eight foot long style statement which blows people's minds in town, but can tour Europe or hustle with aplomb on a curvaceous stretch of road. Try that on almost any other cruiser and you'll beg for mercy – or your money back.

On top of that, this bike looks like a million dollars, featuring the sort of build quality which Honda are renowned for. It glitters like a line of Las Vegas showgirls in rhinestone basques.

Bigger, better and sexier than a Harley.

■ A laugh a minute: this motorcycle is conclusive proof that the Japanese have a sense of humour other than the comic content of gameshows where rabid rodents are let lose on the soft bits of unsuccessful contestants

VITAL STATISTICS

Engine: 1520cc flat six cylinder, four stroke engine with six 28mm carburettors.
Gears: five speed.
Fuel capacity: five gallons.
Dry weight: 309kgs.
Estimated peak power: 100bhp @ 6,500rpm.
Estimated top speed: 125mph.

It was named F6C in Europe in case the word Valkyrie brought Nazi imagery to people's minds.

Ducati

Silk cut smoothie

There have been many attempts to dethrone the mighty Honda VFR750 as king of the sport-tourers, but nothing has come as close in recent years as the sumptuous, totally gorgeous Ducati ST2.

OK, saying that an Italian bike is gorgeous is a bit like saying the Pope is Catholic, but the ST2 is perhaps one of the most significant Latin lovelies to emerge from Bologna in its chequered history. Why? Simple really – it seems to be quite reliable.

Doesn't sound too radical, until you cast your mind back deep in Ducati's past and shudder at the memory of abominations like the 860GTS, the oddly enclosed Paso, the stunning, yet fragile 851 and 888 streetracers, and even – dare I say it – the less than exemplary record of the god-given 916.

For years, Ducati owners who fancied a touring holiday were divided into two dis-

> **❝saying that an Italian bike is gorgeous is a bit like saying the Pope is Catholic❞**

tinct groups; mechanical masochists with a boatload of spares, or passengers on a Shearings 56-seater coach.

But now that Ducati are owned by an American investment firm who are pumping money into the company faster than a frog blowing bubblegum, the ST2 is the first of a whole new generation of motorcycles, machines which can honestly boast the legend "Made In Italy".

In essence the bike is nowt special: a 944cc variant on the traditional 90 degree, four stroke V-twin powers the bike

fairly modestly. But it is so useful, so very liquid, in its power delivery. Then there's the trellis frame and sporty suspension, all of which combine to allow the spirited rider some top fun in the twisties. The ST2 may only do 130mph, but it's the way it develops that speed which stuns you completely.

It is so easy to ride that you just keep on riding it.

When you do eventually tire of deftly flicking this beauty along the best biking roads you can find, then sit back, sip a glass of red wine and admire it, bask in its quiet, subtle glory.

Like a solid-hewn sculpture in silver and alloy, the ST2 shimmers in almost any light, but looks downright spectacular in sunshine. Every curve, each air vent is pure Italiano soul, designed to scythe the air as you boom by – oh yeah, I forgot to mention the noise this baby makes, didn't I?

The great designer Massimo Tamburini once said that "creating a motorcycle is a very passionate act" and if you listen to this machine sing at 8,000–10,000rpm, you will know what he's talking about.

The ST2 rocks.

VITAL STATISTICS

Engine: 944cc 90 degree, four stroke, water cooled, V-twin, SOHC, two valves per cylinder. Gears: six speed. Estimated peak power: 80bhp @ 9,500rpm. Estimated top speed: 130mph.

The ST2 uses no carbs; it has fuel injection, a digital fuel read-out and its own separate production line at the Ducati factory.

Spray on designer stubble

Harley-Davidson Sturgis. If I had to explain, you wouldn't understand. That's what they say at Harley-Davidson when anyone dares to question the enduring appeal of the tractor-like big twins. So I suppose it's just as well that it's me writing this stuff and not the Bubbas and Zekes that carve out each Harley from a solid block of iron, with just a few primitive tools.

I reckon it's pretty straightforward: the Harley-Davidson made in Milwaukee, Wisconsin since they started out in a shed (still standing) in 1902 is the perfect antidote to the 21st century styling and sanitised speed offered by the mainstream (i.e. Japanese) motorcycle industry. In the four-wheeled world the only people with the same philosophy are Morgan who persist with their wood-framed roadsters, equipped with twenties-style sliding pillar suspension. Like Harley, they should have gone bust years ago – instead they've got a six year long waiting list.

I feel I should use this opportunity to put right a misconception about Milwaukee-made motorcycles (try saying that after a six-pack of Schlitz). Most of us think of Harley as providers of righteous rides for bad ass bros, the epitome of which would be this bitchin' (if you'll pardon my Americanism) Sturgis, created to commemorate fifty years of the famous rally to the Black Hills of South Dakota, hence the basic black livery. With its lazy elongated

■ **As cool as an Alaskan outhouse**

and laid back riding position this is a motorcycle with more attitude than a classroom full of 13-year-olds. But for many years Harley Davidson had been the epitome of respectability for the discerning gentleman motorcyclist. What the original Hell's Angels did 'chopperising' their old Harleys, cutting away the excess weight and stretching the handlebars forks and patience of the local police department, was an act of iconoclasm akin to Johnny Rotten snarling his way through *God Save the Queen* in a Vivienne Westwood 'cowboys' T-shirt (ask someone brought up in the seventies to explain).

Of course in the same way that mad old Viv is invited to Buck House garden parties (although no one's actually so daft as to buy her clothes) Harley learned to take these unwashed outlaws into its corporate embrace. Why? Well, it's all about the Benjamins, (100 dollar bills to those of you unfamiliar with street slang). If you've got the bucks they'll build the bike.

So what's the Sturgis like to ride? Well, crap, obviously. Its got no ground clearance, no brakes and generally makes progress like someone who appears on an episode of *Rikki Lake* entitled

> **❝we think of Harley as providers of righteous rides for bad ass bros❞**

'I'm five hundred pounds – and gaining! '

When I rode a Sturgis I was foolish enough to apply the brakes in the wet and got into a sideways slide that would have made Ivan Mauger soil his strides. Still, I loved its big, black beautiful ass, although when you ride any big Harley, you need to learn to lie back with your cowboy boots planted on the forward controls and think of America.

Harley-Davidson

Laverda

Most throbbingly sexy Italian big twin

Years ago, when hairy mammoths and Noddy Holder roamed the earth, Laverda made big, butch bikes. Like the Italian company's combine harvesters, the bikes were heavy, solid-hewn lumps of metal, with controls suitable for gorilla-handed men to wrestle with. They were rough, tough and noisy – proper motorbikes, in fact.

Eventually Laverda went broke, but after another one of those mysterious consortiums of Latin businessmen bought the name, everyone was astonished when the revived concern started producing their new bikes for the 90s, with an updated and enlarged Alpino 500 parallel twin as its engine unit.

It was a bit like buying an Armani ensemble, then discovering that the trousers were from a fifty bob demob suit. The 1990s Laverda 650 was certainly rough, but it wasn't ready for anything over 80mph. Yet within the space of three years, the revitalized Laverda factory had listened to the criticism and honed their machine into something truly special – the 750S.

Resplendent in its funky black and orange paintwork, the machine oozed charisma. Now, however, that beautiful twin spar, Nico Bakker-designed chassis housed an engine which was a worthy match. Pumped up from 650cc to 747cc, the motor gained water cooling, lighter, stronger internals and a better breathing top end. The end result was 82bhp rather than a weedy 65bhp from the old nail, so life became suddenly that bit sweeter.

VITAL STATISTICS

Engine: 747cc water cooled, DOHC, parallel twin, four stroke. Compression ratio: 10.5:1. Gears: six speed. Carbs: None – it has a Weber Marelli fuel injection system instead. Estimated peak power: 82bhp @ 8,000rpm. Brakes: Triple Brembo discs. Estimated top speed: 135mph.

The petrol goes in under the rear seat, which flips up to reveal the filler cap.

The 750S is also a joy to boot through its slinky six speed gearbox, which makes this bike one of the best backroads scratchers money can buy. The revvy twin punts you forwards with poise and precision every time, allowing you to experience the heart and soul of motorcycling – mad bastard cornering. Let's face it, cranking a bike hard into your favourite series of turns is what it's all about, and the Laverda 750S is pure, hard-charging fun.

The other touch which lifts this bike above many Italian machines is quality. Every detail, from the Brembo Goldline brakes – which are, by the way, the size of a builder's estimate – to the elegant tilt of its monoshock gas reservoir, has a symmetry, a wonderfully finished feel about it. This bike looks painstakingly designed, cared for, nurtured by a dedicated factory, not slung together between pizza-eating contests like certain other Italian products.

Motorcycles are such tactile objects that this overall sensation of purity, of total quality in terms of engineering, becomes part of your riding addiction. The 750S is one of those rare machines which rewards real skill, a fluency in operation which sets it, and the rider, apart from the crowd just a touch, and makes you feel that bit more alive.

Coffee bar cool

Norton

What's the worst handling bike you ever rode? Alright, apart from a Harley. Well the answer would probably be the same as it was to the question what's the oldest bike you ever rode? Old bikes are like old people – they require enormous amounts of attention if you want them to work, leak fluids all over the floor at inopportune times and their inevitable death involves huge amounts of expense and inconvenience. And of course neither take corners... without advance warning of at least a fortnight. Trust me I've learned my lesson the hard way on a sucession of golden oldies that bucked, hopped, slapped, understeered and genrally tried to kill me with more enthusiasm than a 23-stone American teenager who hears strange voices in his head and has a dad who works at Uzis-R-Us. People will tell you

"Old bikes are like old people – they require enormous amounts of attention if you want them to work, leak fluids all over the floor at inopportune times and their inevitable death involves huge amounts of expense and inconvenience"

■ **DOMINATOR Style:It's a difficult thing to define, but the Dommie has it in spades.**

that to get the best out of riding old bikes you need to be committed. Well, exactly...

Postwar Nortons are the exception and for that we can thank Mr Rex McCandless and his marvellous double loop Featherbed frame. The Featherbed was thus christened by racer Harold Daniel who was amazed at the sure-footed way that this new machine responded to rider input and remarked that the experience was not unlike cornering in a giant bed full of feathers

and so much better than the old single tube frame known as 'the garden gate' because it looked so much like a garden gate... but with a big engine in the midde and a large wheel at either end. Of course there was no drug testing in those days.

Heading out from the Ace, or The Busy Bee cafes, the 60s Rockers knew how to get the best from a big Brit twin like the Dommie; nail it and hold on tight round the corners. Along with the 650 Bonneville, the Dominator became a definitive icon of rebellion, speed and 'ton-up' power.

VITAL STATISTICS

Engine: 646cc. air cooled parallel twin, four stroke.

Gears: four speed. Carb; Amal Monobloc.

Brakes: Drums front and rear.

Estimated peak power: 40bhp @ 7,000rpm.

Estimated top speed: 105mph.

Dominators can be seen to good effect in the 60s cult movie, *The Leather Boys*.

CBR600

Honda

Best sensible civilized superbike

If Marks and Spencer made motorbikes then this is probably what they'd look like. Except they'd provide a breathable gusset and paint it beige.

Since it was first launched to a suitably appreciative public back in 1987 Honda's benchmark middleweight has defined its class and consistently outsold everything else the same size and shape. Why? Quite simply quality, reliabilty and affordability. In fact the self same attributes that have

made the above mentioned high street retailler such a surefire hit with the underpants buying public. Oh dear, this is not what you were wanting to, hear is it? You're thinking (and maybe you're right), that such hard-headed considerations should not be allowed to dictate the aquisition of an object so romanticised as a motorcycle. Well, you're wrong but I don't blame you. Instead I cite the institutionalised inhabitants of Fantasy Island otherwise known as motorcycling journal-

ists. Fed a diet of free bikes and trips to exotic race track locations in parts of the world only normally visited by German sex tourists they begin to believe that the ability to lay black lines out of superfast corners and hoist the front hoop 45 degrees from the horizontal is the only way to assess any motorcycle's merits... even if it is an Enfield Bullet 350. Back in the real world, many thousands of paying punters have come to realise that the solidly sensible CBR600 offers the complete

■ **The Jack-of-all-trades of modern motorcycling; functional, fun technology**

❝CBR600 offers the complete motorcycling package at a piffling price along with the reassurance that it is a Honda and therefore the chances of it falling to bits are roughly the same as Gazza being elected to the General Synod of the Church of England❞

motorcycling package at a piffling price along with the reassurance that it is a Honda and therefore the chances of it falling to bits are roughly the same as Gazza being elected to the General Synod of the Church of England... or, it seems, getting back in the England squad.

And it's not that sensible either. The original '87 incarnation boasted 83 bhp and an aerodynamically-enhanced top whack of 140mph plus. Ten years on and you're talking more like 100 horses and 150mph. Fit a carb kit and a free-breathing aftermarket exhaust (should you wish

to do so – I couldn't condone that sort of messing with machinery) and you'll see an impressive improvement that the superb chasiss and keen 2-pot sliding stoppers are more than capable of coping with. Yes, its got comfortable accomodation for a pillion. And bungee hook locaters. And a centre stand, for Schwantz's sake. But make no mistake, a well-sorted CBR600 is nothing short of a budget 'blade.

Marks and Spencer? More like Reeves and Mortimer, mate. Slightly surreal but reliably amusing. The Honda CBR600 is what I call a quality item.

Indian

The American Heartland Motorcycle

Who's the Chief? Tasteful decoration on a classic motorcycle

Take a walk down to the nearest street corner and tell me what you see. In fact don't bother because I'll tell you, a procession of mass-produced mediocrity. Hatchback boxes squeezed out like Tupperware by manufacturers so conservative they make Thatcher look like a dangerous radical. Actually Thatcher *was* a dangerous radical but that's probably a subject best left to Ben Elton, a man more deeply entrenched in the eighties than Howard Jones and Simon Le Bon put together (now there's a thought).

But occasionally something slips through the mass-production line that sticks two fingers up to the conventional and drops its pants to show a big hairy butt to the status quo (not Status Quo the band, which would probably be a very bad idea, allegedly). In '59 it was Harley Earl with the fabulously finned chromasorous Cadillac, or Issigonis with the fab and far-out Mini. Back in 1922 it was a chap called Charles B. Franklin and his iconic art deco masterpiece, the Indian Chief.

At one time, and here's a fascinating fact I bet you never knew, the Indian Motocycle (note deliberately dodgy spelling, the pretentious buggers) Company of Springfield Massachusetts was the biggest bike builder in the world. The Chief was the bigger and better-looking brother of the Scout. Power, swiftness, stamina, economy and you'd better

■ The Indian name appeared on increasingly unsuitable machinery including sad sidevalve 250s built by Brockhouse of Southport

believe these white men weren't speaking with a forked tongue. The Scout's 600cc sidevalve v-twin gave it 100 mph potential with cams hotter than the Devil's belch and, remember boys, this was 1920. Thinking about it maybe it should be the Scout here instead of the Chief but, the thing is, I've only ever been pillion on a Scout and when you're thundering around the vertical wooden boards of the Wall of Death, perched on the handlebars like an oversized mascot and praying for your miserable life it's really quite difficult to give an honest assessment.

The day I rode a Chief I found out that things really are different on an Indian. For a start the hand-shift for the three-speed 'box is on the right hand side and the throttle is on the left (they only switched it round in 1950 – three years before they went bust). And I figured out that the perfect celebrity Indian Chief owner would be the giant American that is William (James Tiberius Kirk) Shatner since a motorcycle this flamboyant with its fabulous fully-skirted fenders and giant sprung saddle demands that its rider have an ego as big as that 80 cubic inch engine. Furthermore the combination of the Chief's huge bulk with its rigid rear end and leaf sprung suspension required that he also be the owner of a stout corset – not that I'm implying for one minute that Bill ever employed a beer belly-restraining device. Like I said, the Chief started out in 1922 as a 1000cc sidevalve V-twin and spent the next thirty years getting fatter and slower but more flamboyant, ending its days as a 1300cc, 570lb, rhinestone encrusted and leather–clad dinosaur. Yes this truly was

the Elvis Aaron Presley of motorcycles: an all-time 18-carat tickertape parade American classic.

For such parades the Indian was the preferred choice of US Police forces, as it had a left hand throttle, so that the officer could shoot with his right hand if required.

VITAL STATISTICS

Engine; V-twin sidevalve air cooled 1000cc (1922) 1310cc (1953) Top Speed 75–100mph. Gears: three speed hand shift.

Indian started out in Springfield, Massachusetts in 1901 and ended in Southport. That's not Southport, North Carolina or South, West Virginia but Southport, Lancashire – the seaside resort with the second-longest pier in England – having gone bust in 1953.

❝the combination of the Chief's huge bulk with its rigid rear end and leaf sprung suspension required of the rider that he also be the owner of a stout corset❞

Modrophenia

'O i postman, you've killed me scooter!' For many of you there will be few sights more satisfying in the history of cinema than the one in *Quadrophenia* where Jimmy, the mod muppet and his Lambretta LI 150 end up underneath a side-loading Commer van. The only good scooter is a dead scooter. But hold on a minute. It's not as if the Innocenti Corporation of Milan, Italy – who named their small-wheeled wonder after the river Lamberette, whose banks they built their factory on – was a footnote in the history of the two-wheeled world. In 35 years they produced 17 million vehicles, most of them conventional steel backboned scooters with eager little two-stroke engines and pressed steel panel work, but they also built all kinds of

> ❝The only good scooter is a dead scooter❞

crazy scooter-derived commercial vehicles from the traditional 'just one Cornetto' type trikes to open-topped weirdo wagons.

It's not so well-known that they built a gorgeous 250cc motorcycle that won a couple of races against top-class opposition but which was stuck in a museum after they came to a completely illegal cartel-style agreement with Italy's bike manufacturers that they wouldn't tread on each others toes. Shame they didn't feel the need to do the same with the British bike industry and we might have been spared horrors like the Triumph Tigress and Velocette Viceroy. Scary. Strangely the best Lambretta was probably the last: The GP 200 Electronica. The Electronica bit didn't, as you may have incorrectly assumed, refer to anything so sophisticated as an electric start but merely meant that it didn't have points. And it had a ventilated disc brake which Honda would claim as a technological breakthrough about twenty years

VITAL STATISTICS

Engine: 197cc single cylinder, two stroke, air cooled, with electronic ignition. Estimated peak power; 12bhp @ 7,000rpm. Estimated top speed; 65mph

With the royalties from his first hit single 'Move It' Sir Cliff Richard bought a Lambretta and when production ceased in 1972 the machinery was relocated to a factory in Lucknow, India, where Sir Cliff was born, as plain old Harry Webb, back in 1946.

later. Unfortunately Innocenti were bought out by British Leyland in 1972 so they couldn't sue. Shame. The advertising was classic – alongside a slogan boasting 'The Powerful One' (actually around 12hp) was all sorts of ridiculous sexual innuendo that the Carry On crew would have rejected as too obvious. It looked bloody great though. Bertone – legendary car stylist bloke – was responsible and got it just right. Normally car designers make a complete arse of anything with two wheels, but Bertone got it bob-on with matt black details and suitably psychedelic acid colours. Italian market versions of the GP had a big ink blot on the front legshields because when the drawing arrived from Bertone the great man had dribbled on them and no one at Lambretta had dared to ask if it was deliberate or not. Something similar happened at Aprilia when they commissioned a motorcycle from mad cap French designer fella Phillippe Starck who mistakenly sent them the blueprints for a typically quirky urinal they called the Moto 6.5.

■ **My regeneration: last in a line of classic squat two-wheelers**

Best shark impersonation on two wheels

Suzuki

In one of the most bizarre decisions made by top brass at Suzuki in the late 70s, they gazed upon the squat, almost brutally ugly lines of their new GSX1100 motorcycle, then approached a German company – Target Design – to add some much needed European style to the machine. Yes, that's right, the same Germans who wear lime green pants with a burgundy jacket on breakfast television.

The amazing result of Hans Muth and Jan Fellstrom's midnight oil-burning sessions was the 1981 model Katana; a silver sculpture of pure futurism.

Luckily, the Kat was one bit of futurism which had nowt to do with Gary Numan, men sporting Max Factor, or the cast of *Blake's 7* attempting to act whilst dressed in Bacofoil shoulderpads. In a word, it looked the bollocks – a rakishly long, silver grey blur of speed and power for the cold hearted era of the 80s.

Underneath its sharp suit however, the Kat was essentially the GSX1100, although Suzuki took the opportunity to boost power

VITAL STATISTICS

Engine: 1075cc, DOHC, 16 valve, four cylinder, four stroke. **Gears:** five speed. **Estimated peak power:** 110bhp @ 8,500rpm.
Estimated top speed: 145mph.

The GSX1100S Kat features an electrically operated pop-up headlight.

through a re-worked top end, bigger carbs and a new exhaust system. Around 110bhp spat its way out of that ultra tough engine, which was housed in a Spartan duplex cradle frame, with an anti-dive mechanism on the front forks and hard riding Kayaba rear shocks.

The big Kat was built for high speed travel, mainly in a straight line, which meant the long wheelbase and 19 inch front wheel gave the steering geometry a stability rivalled only by a Japanese bullet train. It was good for 140mph, which was pretty damn fast back in 1981, and the

café racer riding position, complete with the radical looks of the bike, created tremendous interest in the Katana.

Neat touches like the Super Six style dash layout, where both speedo and rev counter ran overlapping each other in an instrument pod, the sidepanel-mounted choke dial and the two-tone, suede seat covering all helped create a distinct identity for the bike, which no other manufacturer dared to even imitate. The Kat 1100 was the first in a range spanning 1,000–550cc variants, each of which had some echoes of the original styling without ever being quite so dramatic.

Whatever you thought of it – and it has since become one of the true cult bikes of the 90s – the Katana was the first real example of European thinking being applied to a Japanese bike; suddenly, the Italians realized that they weren't always going to produce the most trendsetting bikes in the world by right. The Kat was cool.

■ **Kat Scratch Fever: the 1100 Katana is still being made for the retro-crazy Japanese market**

> ❝a rakishly long, silver grey blur of speed and power for the cold hearted era of the 80s❞

27 FJ1200

Best Japanese touring bike of the 80s

The enduring appeal of the FJ1200 Yam can be summed up in one small, yet potent word: grunt.

It's a quality which every good touring bike should have because, let's face it, if you're an Oliver Reed-shaped *bon viveur*, accompanied by a suitably rotund wife, both decked out in the 18 layers of biking kit required to cross the Alps without suffering frostbitten buttocks, then you need all the lowdown pull from the engine that you can get. But the FJ1200 delivers. In terms of grunt, it is probably the most flatulent sumo wrestler of motorcycling.

> **'it is probably the most flatulent sumo wrestler of motorcycling'**

That's no surprise, because the FJ motor is derived from the ancient XS1100 four cylinder unit and features the sort of over-engineered design which the big four Japanese factories loved creating in that era. It grew to 1188cc by the mid-80s, and despite its basic, air cooled, DOHC, across-the-frame layout, soon gained a reputation as one of the most useful sports tourers out in the real world.

Around 125bhp at 8,000rpm doesn't sound that special, but it was the way which the FJ1200 rocketed past traffic – regardless of which gear you happened to be in – which blew the minds of all serious, long distance bikers.

Once the FJ lost its original 16-inch front wheel and skinny forks, it became perhaps the ultimate autobahn blaster. With its cleverly designed half fairing breaking the airflow, the rider was cocooned

---

VITAL STATISTICS

Engine: 1188cc four cylinder, air cooled, transverse, DOHC 16 valve. **Gears:** five speed.
Estimated peak power: 125bhp @ 8,000rpm.
Estimated top speed: 145mph.

The FJ1200 is one of the few modern bikes which has a five gallon fuel tank.

---

in comfort at three-figure speeds, with a 140mph-plus maximum on tap should it be necessary to humiliate some four wheeled joker. The chassis was way above the class standard too. A steel perimeter frame, multi-adjustable forks and an excellent monoshock rear end allowed the rider some fun when the road went bendy.

The only problems with the FJ1200 were the lack of ground clearance and the final drive, which was chain, not shaft. If ever a bike screamed for the convenience of shaft drive through its 10-year life span, the FJ1200 was it, but Yamaha didn't oblige.

But those were the only faults on an otherwise superb machine – a bike which scared the pants off a few BMW engineers, no doubt. It handled decently, toured effortlessly and looked good, even after years of use. Suddenly, the Japanese had cracked the touring bike formula and the FJ1200 had the right stuff, the basic chemistry, that kept people happy.

Planning a biking holiday on an FJ1200 was easy – just grab your Amex card, waterproofs and helmet. Then go.

■ **Torque of the North: greatest living Yorkshireman Jamie Whitham was given an FJ1200 when he signed to Yamaha**

Best Martini People bike

Anytime, anyplace, anywhere. Just grab your helmet, your leathers, and go where you like on this precision masterpiece of a motorcycle. The VFR750 is yet another chillingly well thought out concept by Honda, setting a class standard that other manufacturers still struggle to beat – even after a decade at the top of the sports-tourer division.

So what makes it so special?

It comes back to that old cliché, a blend of the right ingredients. The VFR750 was never the fastest of its type, but it is nevertheless capable of cracking on a bit. Unless you're the type of ingrate who finds 145mph too slow, you won't be disappointed. What's more relevant is that the uncannily smooth, tractable, Vee shaped four cylinder motor always seems to have more in reserve, no matter how hard you accelerate. The VFR doesn't overtake, it simply lopes past lesser vehicles.

The bike also has the sort of easy going fluency in its handling that gives the rider total confidence in the machine. It's not a bike for racing around circuits, but you can soon put the wind up the members of the Nissan Micra living dead as they dither at roundabouts. That comes down to fundamentals being right: a stiff frame, fluid fork action and a well balanced monoshock rear end. You always feel like you are ultimately in charge on the VFR, even at angles of lean which have the footpegs scoring Spirograph patterns in the tarmac.

VITAL STATISTICS

Engine: 781cc four stroke, V-four cylinder, 16 valve, water cooled. **Gears:** 6 speed. **Estimated peak power:** 97bhp @ 10,000rpm. **Estimated top speed:** 145mph.

In the USA, the VFR750 was called the Interceptor.

The Honda also has little detail touches that set it a cut above the hoi polloi of biking. There's dinky hooks for tying luggage

> **The VFR doesn't overtake, it simply lopes past lesser vehicles**

on board, grab-handles for a passenger to cling onto when you hit warp speed, plus a dashboard clock so that you aren't late for that important rotary club dinner.

Everything about the Honda is utterly slick, civilized and finished to the highest standards. It has the engine reliability of a Rolex, the comfortable seating of a touring machine and it emits a slightly muffled version of the sweet soul music which Joey Dunlop's TT winning RVF Hondas used to make in the 80s.

It's clinical yet full of character, and that's what makes people divorce their entire families and move to Pluto rather than part company with the VFR750.

Addictive, powerful and brilliant.

■ **You can ride 500 miles in one day on the VFR and still want to keep on riding**

24 R1100GS

Best hugely insane Trailbike

■ **Gaudy? Only with such a colourful background**

ithout doubt, this is one of the ugliest things to emerge from Germany, ever – which is a scary statement, even if you have seen their breakfast TV shows – yet it is nevertheless one of the best all-round motorcycles you can buy. This is a two wheeled Range Rover: classy, powerful and supremely capable in almost any situation.

Technically, it follows the chassis format which BMW utilised to revive their boxer twins in the early 90s. The engine has the telelever front end, featuring a single shock above an alloy wishbone, and the trick paralever rear, which houses the shaft drive gubbins, bounces up and down, and holds the wheel on too. What all that translates into is a precise steering, agile machine, which is quite capable of giving many so-called sports bikes a run for their money when the going gets bendy. In addition, you sit high up on the GS, holding the ultra-wide handlebars, giving you a terrific view of any insane livestock up ahead, and

letting you feel very much in control.

With typical German thoroughness, this bike is designed with a comfortable dual seat, so you can tour on it, plus a dinky little fly screen, which actually blocks the oncoming breeze more effectively than a taxi driver's buttocks. It's a rider's bike, even though it looks like a mutant Tonka toy.

It also wheelies like a good trailbike should, making it one of the funkiest BMWs in the known universe. Chartered surveyors and their wives called Doreen should perhaps give this one a miss.

> **This is one of the ugliest things to come out of Germany, ever**

■ **BMW Style: It may look like a Tonka toy, but the R1100GS is definitely a rider's bike**

AGUSTA F4

Fast by Fellini

MV Agusta and Ferrari. It's an obvious connection to make for all sorts of reasons not least that each marque was essentially the grand passion of one man. Enzo was Ferrari the same way that Count Domenica Agusta was MV Agusta. Each gave much more than his name to the exotic and beautiful racing machine that bore his name because, of course, they both cared little about the boring business of making road-going motorcycles. It was racing and winning that obsessed them to the end.

And this is where the connection comes apart because, well, Ferrari just don't win enough, I mean the cars look lovely and everything – all that blood red paint – but, to be brutally frank, they ain't won nothing since 1983. Maybe the Tifosi might be better switching their allegiance to Manchester City.

All MV Augusta ever did was win between 1949 and 1976 when a combination of two stroke technology and big business interests finally brought the evocative scream of the four stroke racing engine to an end at GP level.

But Count Agusta, Agostini, Hailwood, Bonera Arturo Magni and all the other backroom boys did the marque proud in those years. They scored 256 Grand Prix wins and took 38 riders and 37 constructors' championships. They raced singles, twins, triples, fours and almost stole some of the glory from Honda with a beautifully compact six cylinder 250.

Above all, they oozed charisma, panache and Italian brio. Now, like the sequel to a dreamlike Fellini movie, MV Agusta is back, courtesy of Cagiva, with a modern, transverse four cylinder four stroke, outrageous styling and a mouth watering chassis.

Like so many other Latin motorcycles, the new MV is a bold statement, a challenge to bikers everywhere and more especially, to the mainstream Japanese manufacturers; the best is coming back.

At 25 grand a bike, let's just hope that it is some kind of ultimate.

■ Exhausts simply had to routed under the seat; pure Italian style

> **❝outrageous styling and a mouth watering chassis❞**

VITAL STATISTICS

Engine: 748cc four cylinder, transverse, four stroke, four valve head engine.
Estimated peak power: 140bhp @ 10,500rpm.
Estimated top speed; 165mph
Dry weight: 193kgs.
Fuel capacity: 18 litres.

Cagiva – for reasons best known to themselves – once owned Jawa-CZ.

'outrageous styling and a mouth watering chassis'

■ MV heritage: The factory have already decided that Ago is having the first one

VTR100 FIRESTORM

Best 21st century Brough Superior

Honda

The BSA Bantam – a quintessentially British example of antique English iron – was of course German. As British as the Royal Family in fact. Aprilia's Latin love machine, the RS250, is about as Italian as Billy Connolly's beard – being largely based on Suzuki's equally insane little stroker the RGV250. And of course the Yamaha Virago is built by the Clangers out

❝the Yamaha Virago is built by the Clangers out of space junk❞

of space junk in a factory next door to the soup dragon's bungalow

But I digress. The Honda VTR1000, known as the Firestorm to its friends, was assumed to be nothing less than a Japanese built version of the other sporting V-twins built

in Bologna. Making it available in a choice of either fire engine red or egg yolk yellow didn't do much to disabuse anyone of that opinion. Still it seemed like a great idea on the face of it. Traditional Latin attributes in the artistic interpretation department would be combined with the oriental aptitude for the compulsory and technical merit sections. Straight six scores all around mate.

It was a great idea and no surprise that most of the Japanese manufacturers all thought of it at around the same time. Yamaha were first with their TRX850 but only because it was the motorcycling equivalent of Johnny Cash's Cadillac being made using components from every other motorcycle in the Yamaha range as well as the odd bit off a golf buggy, snow mobile and chainsaw.

■ **Fave Rave: I like it so much I nearly bought the company**

VITAL STATISTICS

Engine: 998cc V-twin, four stroke, water cooled, four valve head.
Claimed peak power: 105bhp @ 9,000rpm.

The best selling bike in Italy is a V-twin built by Honda. But it ain't no sports bike, it's that chromosexual cruiser for chaps-wearing cappuccino cowboys: the VT600C Shadow.

The Honda Firestorm and Suzuki TL1000S both appeared at the beginning of 1997 and the sensible money was on the big Suzi. Quite simply it looked wilder than a night out with Stan Collymore; mad, bad, but, as it turned out, dangerous to know. "125hp at the back wheel" said Suzuki with a big stupid grin on their faces. "Ten Grand says it doesn't" retorted the disbelieving Ducati importer. He almost choked on his cappuccino when the TL clocked 123hp in independent tests. Suzuki had chased the dragon of pure speed and mainlined on massive horsepower but like most junkies they forgot about the other important stuff. The suspension couldn't cope and the British bike press treated the story in the same balanced and reasonable way that the tabloids had tackled BSE.

The Tl1000 was labelled the mad cow of motorcycling. In contrast the Firestorm is still with us and in these days of accelerated development without so much as a decal being different. So the riding position is still relaxed, the styling restrained and the output from the 90 degree 1000cc v-twin still stuck at 105hp – an almost embarrassingly limp figure when exhibited alongside the bulging big numbers of the 130–140 hp new boys on the superbike block. But the most telling statistic on the Firestorm's CV is the 70ft/lbs of torque it pumps out at

6,500rpm. So it struggles to crack 150mph when the others are bursting through 170mph with ease. So what? Spend any time at speeds double the existing British limit and you'll end up in the paper under one of two headings: Speed Crazed Beast Caged For 140mph Rampage or Maniac Biker Killed In Terror Carnage. And no one wants that. What you do want is the sort of midrange oomph that will propel you from one bend to the next like you've got an Exocet up your arse and that is exactly what the Firestorm does. Of course it doesn't look or sound nearly as good as a Ducati 916 and it trades the raw thrills on offer from the Italian stallion for an altogether more civilized experience. But then it was never intended to be a Ducati clone – lazy journalists just assumed it would be. Truth is it's much closer in spirit to the sort of V-twin powered gentlemen's grand tourer we used to be so good at.

The VTR1000 Firestorm is nothing less than a 21st century Brough Superior or Vincent Black Shadow. But then I would say that, I ride one…

WLA45

Best warhorse for kicking ass

Take a good long look at this motorcycle. Now there are a lot of things you could say about the Harley-Davidson WLA – that it is typically big and tough with a heavy frame, rigid rear end and indestructible girder forks – and that while its air cooled 750cc (45 cu in) sidevalve lump was never going to win any races – except perhaps with heavily-armoured ordnance of the Wehrmacht – it would just keep on running. But one thing you would never say about the WLA (that 'A' was for Army) is that it is pretty. Handsome perhaps in the square-jawed John Wayne manner, but there have been better looking bikes.

Still, if you were living in occupied Europe in World War Two then one of these ridden by gum-chewing GIs or khaki-clad Tommies (the British Army bought the WLA in big numbers) was the most beautiful sight you ever saw since they were often the first allied presence in occupied territory which is how it got its nickname – 'The Liberator'.

And that ain't all. As well as freeing Europe from the yoke of Nazi oppression the WLA kept The Harley-

Davidson Motor Co. out of the bankruptcy court. When it first appeared in the twenties the W series had been a bit of a bad joke. In fact it looked so sad next to the splendid Indian Scout – which was a good 20 mph faster – that Harley took it off the market and sorted it out with new flywheels, aluminium pistons and re-circulating oil lubrication. They

VITAL STATISTICS

Engine: 45 degree air-cooled V-twin 750cc (45 cu in) **Power output:** 20hp **Gears:** three speed hand-shift.

Harley's sidevalve '45' stayed in production for 43 years. Debuting in 1929 its final task was turning the twin rear wheels of Harley's Servicar – a three wheel delivery vehicle for truly cool ice cream men.

> **'if you were living in occupied Europe in World War Two then one of these ridden by gum-chewing GIs or khaki-clad Tommies (the British Army bought it in big numbers) was the most beautiful sight you ever saw'**

submitted it to the US Army for testing in 1936 and the rest is history. A History written by us, in the free world, just think without it, we could have all been forced to ride BMW boxers, cultivate dodgy facial hair and wear brown leathers.

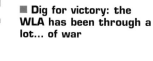

■ **Dig for victory: the WLA has been through a lot... of war**

GOLD WING 21

Best way to tour the world

> 'Middle aged couples have been known to hold line dancing sessions in the top box '

■ It's not gold and it hasn't got wings. Any bigger and it would need a police escort on a motorway

This is a Parker Knoll recliner on wheels, an armchair view of the world as it unravels beneath your wheels of steel. The 1500cc flat six engined Big Daddy of touring bikes will glide along all day at 90mph, whilst you and your passenger enjoy the many on-board gadgets. This bike reaches US motorhome levels of style, comfort and luxury, but is one of the most functional motorcycles ever built too.

Starting life in 1975 as a flat four 1,000 flagship sports-tourer for Honda, it soon grew in size through 1100cc, then 1200cc, with the 1.5 litre mothership Aspencade model arriving in the late 80s. Like so many other Honda motorcycles, it

evolved into the ultimate expression of its particular type. The Wing got smoother, its tape deck and radio got clearer sound, the seating mirrored that of a Mercedes limousine, and the weather protection grew wider than a set of barn doors. It even has a heating vent system.

Because the weight of this land leviathan topped 800lbs, it also got a reverse gear – which works off the starter motor button. Like a bear in the woods, you can park a Gold Wing wherever you like.

With deeply practical values like the way the bike carries its weight low, its shaft drive rather than messy chain, and its Albert Hall-sized luggage capacity, the Wing

is the only way to travel if you really do insist on taking the kitchen sink. Middle-aged couples have been known to hold line dancing sessions in the top box at the back of this bike.

Around the world in 80 days?

No problem on a Gold Wing.

VITAL STATISTICS

Engine: 1500cc, water cooled, six cylinder. Gears: six, including reverse which is selected by special lever on the left side-panel. Estimated peak power: 100bhp @ 5,500rpm. Estimated top speed: 115mph.

Rallies for Gold Wing owners are known as "Wing Dings" or "Treffens."

103

20 ZX9R NINJA

Kawasaki

Raging bull

You meet the nicest people on a Honda. Sensible, budget conscious types go for Suzukis. Posers will show up down the wine bar on a Harley or Ducati 916 perhaps. But without doubt, nutters ride Kawasakis, especially 900cc Kawasakis which rocket from standstill to 150mph in around 14 seconds. The ZX9R is the Jake La Motta of motorcycling; a donut-stuffing, wife-beating, foul-mouthed mother of a motorbike, which will tear your head off in an insane whirlwind of speed and power. Great. Designed by the same team at Kawasaki which brought the world the original Z1900 (unlikely, I know; surely they should all be out playing virtual reality crown green bowls by now?) the first generation ZX9R was a slightly porky thing – terrifically powerful, but ultimately too slow in the corners to trouble the quick guys on Fireblades, or even a ZXR750 Kawasaki for that matter.

But in 1998, the ZX9R came good. With a meaner, Lena Zavaroni-type figure,

■ True to the Kawasaki spirit, the **ZX9R** really begs to be thrashed above **9,000rpm** to get the best from it

> ❝a donut-stuffing, wife-beating, foul-mouthed mother of a motorbike, which will tear your head off in an insane whirlwind of speed and power❞

■ **The ZX9R is probably the most improved superbike of the 90s**

(astonishingly, the new ZX9R shed some 70lbs of dry weight over its forerunner) yet more bhp at the back wheel and much more rakish looks, the big Kwacker was ready to have a serious pop at the Honda Fireblade for the first time. The new Kawasaki handled with real agility, yet also possessed that same uncanny stability at berserko speeds which the 'Blade seemingly claimed as a birthright back in 1992. It all adds up to one of the most balanced and planted motorcycles on the road today, which is a bit of cliché I know, but very true. It's one of those bikes which allows you to make a mistake at some ridiculous speed, then get away with it. But at the heart of the experience, there's still this mad rush of sheer power, just waiting on the naughty side of 7,000rpm to catapult you beyond the next town. The ZX9R Ninja gets right back to what made Kawasaki a great name in motorcycling. It's a rough and ready streetfighter, always game for a bit of a punch-up if some whippersnapper fancies his chances. From the tip of its unbelievably loud titanium exhaust pipe, to the shark-like prow of its fairing, the Ninja simply oozes speed. The bonus is that the Kawasaki can cut up rough with a dash of finesse; it's a gentleman thug.

19 R1200C

Best Blade Runner future bike

Conclusive proof that the Germans not only have a sense of humour, but actually have some taste too – despite inflicting Kraftwerk upon us. The BMW R1200C is probably best known as the James Bond bike from *Tomorrow Never Dies*, and this is indeed a piece of the future made metal by some twisted Teutonic genius.

Featuring the 90s BMW boxer-style, flat twin four stroke engine, you might think

> **'A piece of the future made metal by some twisted Teutonic genius'**

VITAL STATISTICS

Engine: 1170cc two cylinder, four valve head, direct injection, four stroke.
Gears: Five speed.
Brakes: ABS anti-lock disc braking all round.
Estimated peak power: 61bhp @ 5000rpm.
Estimated top speed: 110mph.

With a seat height of under 30", the R1200C is particularly suitable for shorter riders with a scary turn of mind.

■ **The Best Badass Bitchin' Bike Built by Bavarians**

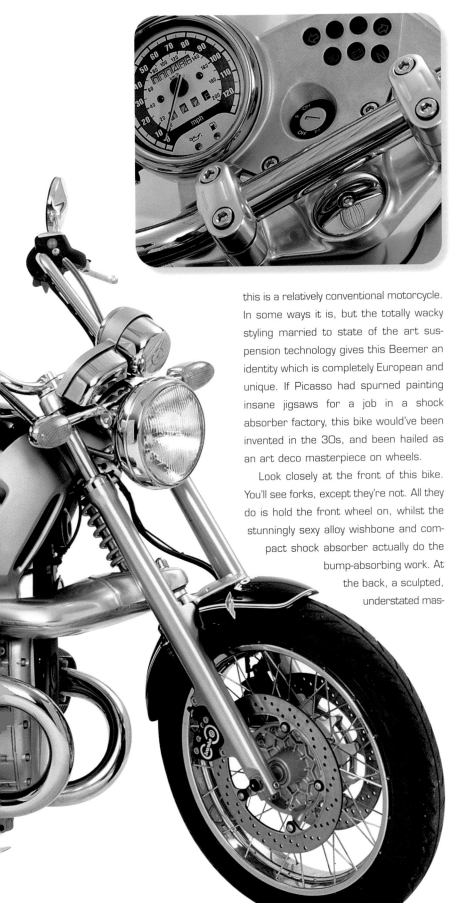

terpiece of extruded alloy does a similar job, and also houses the drive shaft. Both bits of metal act as stressed members to hold the engine in place too.

So brilliant, yet beautiful to look at. What this techno trickery does is give the BMW R1200C a distinct handling advantage over the average lardyguts cruiser, enabling you to ride beyond 70mph and then take a corner without engaging oncoming traffic in a quick session of the Lambada. Cute touches like the flip-up pillion seat – which forms a handy backrest – the deeply sexy chrome and those heavenly hot rod exhausts all add glamour.

Achtung baby, let's ride this 21st Century toy.

this is a relatively conventional motorcycle. In some ways it is, but the totally wacky styling married to state of the art suspension technology gives this Beemer an identity which is completely European and unique. If Picasso had spurned painting insane jigsaws for a job in a shock absorber factory, this bike would've been invented in the 30s, and been hailed as an art deco masterpiece on wheels.

Look closely at the front of this bike. You'll see forks, except they're not. All they do is hold the front wheel on, whilst the stunningly sexy alloy wishbone and compact shock absorber actually do the bump-absorbing work. At the back, a sculpted, understated mas-

■ It may look like a cross between a Harley and a Henry Moore sculpture, but luckily it doesn't ride like one

18 RSV 1000 MILLE

The most compact and bijou Italian 1,000cc V-Twin

Aprilia

For over 10 years, Aprilia built a reputation on banzai, banshee two strokes which allowed Latin teenagers to descend upon urban piazzas like a swarm of angry, acne-scarred wasps, frantically racing every other road user in a bid to gas the population in a sweaty fog of testosterone.

They weren't a pretty sight, but their Aprilia bikes were generally beautifully put together, as the Noale factory sought to dominate the lucrative Italian 125cc market. The Aprilia 125 Extrema, for example, has a front disc brake so stunningly gorgeous, so graspingly powerful, that dentists use it to pull the teeth from doe-eyed, 19-year-old, Latin girlie sex-kittens who gently whimper in pain.

Sorry, where were we? Oh yes, the Aprilia RSV1000 is the first big bike from a company which had previously regarded a Pegaso 650 four stroke single as a large capacity sports-tourer. Yet it is nevertheless a physically tiny 1000cc motorcycle.

At its heart, there is a sweet 60 degree, four stroke, DOHC, V-twin, developed by the factory themselves. That's a first for Aprilia, as they usually rely on off-the-shelf engines from other manufacturers. It's a modern, fuel injected motor, using a computer engine management chip, two spark plugs per cylinder, and balancer shafts inside the cases to absorb some of the natural vibration a big Vee makes.

Setting the motor's twin

cylinders at 60 rather than 90 degrees (as Ducati do) keeps the engine short in length. Using dry sump lubrication also shrinks a little more from the overall dimensions, because Aprilia wanted this baby to be very, very short in the wheelbase.

The reason? Handling. This bike is designed to corner faster than Maradona on the old Bolivian marching powder, with its twin spar alloy frame, monoshock rear end, 43mm upside down forks and 1415mm wheelbase.

The rear swingarm, with its curvaceous bracing sweeping along the top of it, is simply a piece of art – and it works. The chassis has all the rigidity you'll ever need, even at 150mph.

It also looks mouth-wateringly good, as all Italian motorcycles should. The traditional Aprilia blue and red colour scheme serves as the finishing touch on a sculpted fairing, all scoops and vents in the right places. The shape of the RSV suggests speed, aggression, control. In the final analysis, it's a rider's bike, pure and simple.

The very essence of motorcycling.

■ **Run of the Mille: nice, but no real competition for Ducati**

VITAL STATISTICS

Engine: 997cc, 60 degree, V-twin, four stroke, DOHC, water cooled. **Carbs:** None, it has Digital fuel injection. **Gears:** 6 speed. **Estimated peak power:** 128bhp @ 9,250rpm.
Estimated top speed: 165mph.

The RSV1000 has three headlamps.

❝Aprilia wanted this baby to be very, very short in the wheelbase❞

SUPER BLACKBIRD

Honda

1100X Best impersonation of a stealth bomber

Honda admitted that the name of this bike – and its dark, brooding bodywork – were inspired by one of the meanest looking warplanes of the 60s, the USAF Blackbird spy plane. That drove the engineers at the world's biggest bike maker to strive for the ultimate aerodynamic motorcycle shape, stretching the performance envelope ever closer to the mythic 200mph figure.

Yes Auntie Mabel, that's correct, I said 200mph.

The fact that the Blackbird tops out somewhere in the mid-170s is no great disappointment, because this machine is so devastatingly casual in its acceleration beyond 100mph that the rider can sometimes imagine that the bike is going to become airborne imminently. Power simply floods through this motorcycle, turbine smooth and eerily silent, except for the ever increasing wind roar.

But wait, the Blackbird is more than a guided missile. For a start, it takes corners – all sorts of corners – like a rock star takes to chasing big blonde girls with small brains. There's no fuss or drama, the Blackbird merely impresses the hell out of the rider with its steady, fluent capability. Each time you accelerate out of a corner at some insane speed, all you can think about is how much faster you should've taken the bend. It is uncannily self-assured at speed.

> ❝ Faster pussycat, kill, kill ❞

■ **Honda powerhouse: you'll pull over 100mph on this bike without even thinking about it**

VITAL STATISTICS

Engine: 1137cc transverse four cylinder, water cooled, four stroke. **Gears:** six speed. **Estimated peak power:** 164bhp @ 10,000rpm. **Estimated top speed:** 175mph.

Although it has almost an extra 100bhp, the Blackbird weighs around the same as the original CB750 Honda.

You can also carry a passenger or sling some luggage on the Blackbird, then travel in some comfort at an average speed which rail commuters in the South East can only fantasize about. Where you go and how fast is your business, but rest assured that the Blackbird will get you there. The bike moves through traffic with devastating ease – a tiny, tiny, flick of the throttle and cars are totally humiliated in any sort of acceleration contest.

So this is the biggest, swoopiest commuter bike on the roads. It can catapult you into the next galaxy, and it tours remarkably well. Like so many other Hondas, it is a consumate all-rounder which makes you feel more relaxed than Des Lynam whenever you ride it.

Best of all, the more you ride it, the sooner you discover the true talent the Blackbird has in its dark, metallic grey paintwork; it is almost invisible to traffic policemen. The conservative looks of the bike are a stark contrast to some of the brighter rocketships out there, some of which appear to have been painted by computer-game-addled seven-year-olds let loose in a crayon factory.

On the Blackbird, you're on a perfect stealth mission. Faster pussycat, kill, kill.

Suzuki

Best sexy retro

Come with me now as we travel back through time to the early 80s, when grotesque and dangerous dinosaurs like Kajagoogoo roamed the plains and men rode bikes without fairings. Then, we laughed at rain, hail or killer wasps flying arse forwards into our mouths, on bikes like GPz750s, Suzuki GSX1100s and Honda CB900Fs.

Were we completely insane?

Most likely, but there was an undeniable sense of excitement in piloting those overweight behemoths along the road. For car drivers, it's probably a bit like looking back to the "great" British sports cars of the 70s like the MGBGT, or the… er… Triumph Spitfire. Wind in the hair, deafening noise, horrible lack of brakes, small boys in the park with jumpers for goalposts – marvellous, wasn't it?

Of course, nowadays you can have that authentic retro experience without the sheer pain of actually riding a weedy forked,

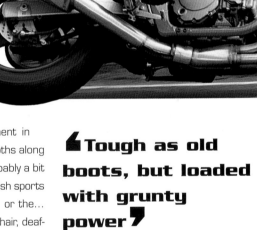

VITAL STATISTICS

Engine: 1157cc, transverse four cylinder, four stroke, air cooled. Gears: five speed. Estimated peak power: 105bhp @ 9,500rpm. Estimated top speed: 135mph.

The 1200 Bandit is the most popular choice for cheap tuners – simply changing the exhaust gains 15bhp.

> ❝Tough as old boots, but loaded with grunty power❞

underpowered, ill-handling brute of a bike. All you need to do is go out and purchase a Suzuki Bandit 1200 at a knockdown price.

What you get for your wedge is one of the best all time top fun backroads blasters ever made. It features a stonking engine lifted from the 80s classic sportster, the GSXR1100. Tough as old boots, but loaded with grunty power.

Then you get triple drilled disc brakes, with four piston calipers at the front that stop you dead in your tracks like a Tory candidate north of Birmingham. Add half a fairing, a soft seat and a decent fuel range – suddenly we are in great all-rounder ter-

■ **The best value retro bike you can get your hands on; fast, fun and cheap**

ritory and it even looks pretty good. Well, it does in red anyway.

The Bandit wheelies, it tours, it commutes. It might even get your whites whiter than Daz can, I don't know. What I do know is that this top fun motorbike makes you want to get out there whenever the sun dares to shine, and go. Go anywhere, in fact.

The bike that started the retro trend in the early 90s was the Kawasaki Zephyr, which we all thought was great at the time but now seems little more than a foul memory. Suzuki realized that "born again" bikers deserve as much value in their retro package as humanly possible – otherwise, they'll forget about motorcycles and go and buy an MG from some salesman with a dodgy haircut.

And nobody in their right mind wants to see that sort of thing, do they?

15 XR750

Harley-Davidson

The Powerslider

You are looking at the most successful racing motorcycle in the world, ever. Legendary racing greats like the MV Agusta four-cylinder GP machines of the fifties and sixties, Yamaha TZs in the seventies and eighties and even Ducati Superbikes in the nineties can only glance enviously at the racing record of this tail-sliding, head-shaking shale-spitting superstar.

The XR750 started its winning ways over twenty-five years ago and so far shows no sign of stopping. Back in the twenties Harley-Davidson ruled motorcycle racing stateside. By that I don't mean they achieved consistent success out on the track, I mean they were in charge on account of the fact that they ran the American Motorcyclists Association, which had been abandoned by the racers who set it up. Hey, that's racers for you – the attention span of an impatient goldfish. While the rules didn't actually disqualify motorcycles that didn't come from 'somewhere beginning with M', they didn't stop far off because, as everyone knew, overhead valves were a sign of communist activity and parallel twins as sure a sign as any of Satanic worship.

So it wasn't until the sixties that the upstart Limeys with their Triumphs, Nortons and BSA (hey buddy, lightweight bikes, lightweight country) managed to get a say with the AMA. And in 1968 the 53-year-old rule that limited machines sporting those new-fangled overhead valves to 500cc (i.e. British bikes) but allowed side valve racers up to 750cc (ie. motor sick-

■ **Mastered by men of iron called Cal, Jay or Mert**

les made the American way) was abolished. Harley-Davidson's immediate reaction was to lose – big time. In the full-on, flat-out world of flat tracking those first iron-engined XR750s proved to be as durable as the jet engine of a Boeing 747 at full thrust when you introduce a large Canada goose.

The solution was quite simple: in

1972 they were equipped with alloy cylinders and heads and a couple of Japanese Mikuni carburettors (goddam un-American if you ask me). Ridden by square jawed heroes like Cal Rayborn – a man so cool and hard he made Steve McQueen look like Charles Hawtrey – and Jay Springsteen (no relation to the twat out of Jamiroquai), the XR has proved more or less invincible. In fact Yamaha found that the only way to beat it was to create the scariest racing motorcycle of all time by forcing their nsane 2-stroke TZ750 road race engine into a slap-happy track machine. Ridden by the god-like Kenny Roberts, it won one race but, concerned that mere mortals would be tempted to take on this satanic stallion, the AMA banned big two strokes from the ovals.

There was a road-going version called the XR100, and with 100 horsepower it is probably the quickest roadbike Harley-Davidson ever offered (excepting the officially-endorsed efforts of Eric Buell). It looked good too, with high-level pipes, twin carbs (Italian Dellortos) and a fastback seat unit. Of course it didn't sell, so Harley dropped it. Somewhere in America someone is racing an XR750, stuffing it into a 100mph turn and, you know what, he's probably going to win.

VITAL STATISTICS

Engine: 45-degree air-cooled 750cc v-twin. **Power output:** a black art usually around 100hp. **Brakes:** Brakes are for candy asses and fags. Maybe one at the back to get the tail out.

Of the 200 XR750s with iron top ends built to qualify for what was ostensibly a street-bike series, 100 were scrapped to prevent privateers racing them with inevitable and unpleasant consequences. If they'd put them in storage those bikes would now be worth a fortune.

‘overhead valves were a sign of communist activity’

The long distance runner ■

Moto Guzzi

Remember when sex was safe and motorcycles were dangerous?

So say the bumper stickers on the back of Southern boys' pick up trucks, who also advocate preserving the rights of schizophrenic schoolkids to have access to machine guns.

Mind you, I can quite easily recall a time when finding a Japanese superbike with reassuringly powerful brakes and responsive handling was about as likely as finding yourself stood next to Stephen Fry in the front row of a wet T-shirt competition. Therefore I can understand why back in '76 people bought the Moto Guzzi 850 Le Mans.

Right let's get one thing straight shall we? The 850 Le Mans was no eccentric

> **‘built by Italian artisans in a soot blackened factory’**

VITAL STATISTICS

Engine: 843cc V-twin four stroke air cooled. Estimated peak power: 70bhp @ 7,000rpm.
Estimated top speed: 125mph.
Dry weight: 205kgs.
Fuel capacity: 20 litres.

The Mk III Le Mans featured a sixteen inch front wheel, which made it steer like a pig on rollerblades

contraption that offered dubious delight for the terminally quirky. This was a one of the first superbikes of the modern era. In a straight line its 70hp made it as quick as a Suzuki GS1000. That's right, a bike built by Italian artisans in a soot-blackened factory straight out of a Dickens novel with a transverse V-twin tractor engine could match the finest four cylinder multivalve motor of the day. There were two reasons why this was possible: Guilio Carcano

and Lino Tonti. They extracted class-leading performance from the unlikeliest lump in motorcycling. The mysteries of handling were then uncharted by the Japanese. By contrast, the Le Mans had stuff like weight distribution and unsprung weight well sorted. Then there were those infamous linked brakes. Tugging on the lever only operated the right hand disc only while the left hand front and back were worked by pedal. Everyone else will tell you that they didn't work but I've spoken to one of the few to race a Le Mans with any kind of success and he told me he disconnected them in the dry but reconnected them in the wet. He told me that once, the lever had fallen off halfway through a race leaving him stamping on the pedal like a church organist on a amphetamimnes

Looking at Moto Guzzi's outdated, underdeveloped range today it's easy to forget that fifty years ago they were building wildly innovative but consistently successful race bikes. The 850 Le Mans was a product of the same obstinacy, belief and passion. It would be a real shame if it were the last of the great Guzzis.

■ **One tough engine, originally designed for use in a lorry**

13 BONNEVILLE 650 T120

Triumph

Best old rocker's bike

Bonneville.

There's still something magic about the name, isn't there, even after all these years. When this sporty 650cc parallel twin first saw the light of day, Bill Haley was still almost hip, women wore seamed stockings made from gravy browning and Vimto cost just fourpence a pint. We are talking 1950s here daddy-o, although the era when the Bonny truly ruled the roads was the swinging 60s.

The lean, lowdown look of the Bonneville set it apart from contemporary British stodge like Ajay jampots, bathtub Triumphs and their festering ilk. This was an evolutionary leap forward for Edward Turner's original Speed Twin design, complete with a "cammy" engine, sexy exhausts and the wildest handling this side of a dodgem. The Bonneville was a 110mph fairground waltzer ride for lads with too much Brylcreem and a chip on their shoulder – and they loved it.

Not surprising, really, as the 650cc four stroke motor provided the basis for all sorts of tuning malarkey, plus it begged to be slotted into the benchmark Norton Featherbed frame for the ultimate coffee bar racer. That became known as a Triton, invented by one Dave Degens, which is another story altogether, but the Bonny remained perhaps the favourite big British twin of the times for three simple reasons: it looked cool, it sounded meaty, but above all else, it was fast.

You would never see "Fartbeat's" PC Nick

> **built for picking up fast ladies in short skirts with big bee-hives at Friday Night dances**

Rowan of the 60s astride a Bonny, because it was too much like a good time to allow village coppers toys like these. No, a vile Velocette two stroke barely capable of catching a lively donkey was far more suitable.

The Bonneville was a bike built for picking up fast ladies in short skirts with big bee-hives at Friday night dances, or ripping along on the first non-speed-limited motorways. It was also great for burning down

■ **The boys are back in town… and they're riding their bonnies**

from the Ace caff with your mates to Brighton or Margate for a bank holiday rumble with Italian-suited weasels on Lambrettas.

The Bonneville 650 became a 750 in due course, and struggled along into the 1980s before an embarrassed nation finally nailed its oil-stinking coffin shut.

But way before then, in the days of glory, the Bonneville provided more moments of pure escapism than all the hash in Ladbroke Grove, and carved itself a place in biking history. An icon of British steel, noise and power. Even today, you can still hear a whole generation of old men in flat hats begin a sentence, "I used to have a bike once, it was a Triumph Bonneville…"

VITAL STATISTICS

Engine: 649cc four stroke, twin cylinder, air cooled. Gears: four speed. Estimated peak power: 46bhp @ 6,500rpm. Estimated top speed: 110mph.

The first Production class TT race was won by John Hartle on a Bonny in 1967, at an average speed of 97mph.

NSR500 V4

The Ultimate GP Bike?

When Honda came back to 500cc Grand Prix racing in the early 1980s, they made a fundamental – with a definite accent on mental – mistake: they tried to win on a four stroke. The NR500 was a V4 four stroke, mini-wheeled, monocoque chassis project which fitted into Honda's corporate philosophy, but had no business out on a racetrack. In short, Honda got stuffed. Big time.

So they went back to the drawing board and came up with the NS500 triple. Punting out over 150bhp, it was a fire-breathing V4 shaped, reed valve induction two stroke, which had a tendency to spit its back end sideways, and the front wheel

> **❛This bike would kill you within half a lap unless you were possessed of an unreal talent❜**

skywards, when the power came on strong. If there were any doubts about the level of skill required to tame this scream-ing beast, they were surely dispelled when Wayne Gardner – an Australian racer with balls of case-hardened steel and a will to win just this side of disturbed – failed to tame Fast Freddie's V4 missile.

Yet Gardner became the first Australian to win the blue riband 500cc GP crown in 1987 aboard an NSR500 which was a long way off becoming the apparently dominant GP bike it is today. However, it was another unassuming, "no worries" type of Aussie who brought the NSR500

VITAL STATISTICS

Engine: 499cc two stroke, water cooled, reed valve induction V4. Estimated peak power: 190bhp @ 12,500rpm. Dry weight; 286lbs. Estimated top speed; 200mph.

The NSR needs a seven gallon fuel tank to cover the average 65 mile GP race.

to a dominant position in GP racing; Mick Doohan.

In 1992 Doohan began the season on the 'Big Bang' NSR500. This gave the rear tyre an easier life under hard acceleration, which translated into a faster drive out of one bend and onwards to the next. Suddenly, Doohan was winning GPs as if Rainey and the rest were on 250s, although a big crash in 1992 put the championship out of reach. From 1994, onwards however, Doohan and the NSR500 roadshow swept the board. Then he did something only

a champion can contemplate. He went back to the "Screamer" model in 1997. It was possibly the bravest gamble in GP racing history, but it paid off. Lighting up the tyre as he went, sliding the beast across the GP circuits of the world like it was a kid's skateboard, Mick Doohan makes handling 190bhp of bucking Honda look easy. It isn't. It's a vicious animal of a bike and when celebrities answering inane interviews in sad "lad" magazines claim that their dream is to "ride Mick Doohan's NSR500" they are talking out of their tiny, baboon-arsed brains. This bike would kill you within half a lap unless you were possessed of an unreal talent. That primal fear, the raw, explosive motorhead beauty, is what makes the NSR500 per-haps the ultimate fairground white-knuckle ride in motorcycling.

Awesome.

■ **Doing the business: Michael Doohan has rear-wheel-steered the NSR500 to four world titles**

MV AGUSTA 500 FOUR

The fastest fire engine

The most powerful mythology in the four-wheeled world has been built around the marque named after its creator 'Il commendatore' Enzo Ferrari. People employed to express an opinion on these things will often comment on the similarities between the Prancing Horse of Maranello and the bike builders from just down the road in Bologna, Ducati. There are all sort of reasons why this should make sense but I think these people must have short memories because not so long ago Italy once had a manufacturer of motorcycles far more worthy of the accolade: MV Agusta.

Just like Enzo, Count Domenico Agusta was obsessed with racing and winning. And if there was one thing the glorious 'Gallatre Fire Engines' were good at, it was winning. Between their first forays in 1950 to the mid-seventies, before the death of the don and the onslaught of 2-strokes from the East, they enjoyed success unparalleled in the history of motorcycle racing: 275 Grand Prix wins, 37 constructors championships. And you thought Mickey Doohan must be getting bored with spraying the celebratory champers. The

■ In a word, horny – and you haven't even heard it yet

" the only championship they didn't dominate was the 50cc because the Count felt the tiddlers were beneath the dignity of his aristocratic thoroughbreds "

only championship they didn't dominate was the 50cc because the Count felt the tiddlers were beneath the dignity of his aristocratic thoroughbreds.

So how did he do it? Quite simply he waved his chequebook. The story of the Count and his scarlet and silver racers is

a romantic tale that speaks to the sentimental soul of motorcyclists down the years. A self-made man who dragged himself and his business out of the rubble of post-war industry and made enough money to take on the world. His way.

I think we underestimate the Italians. The stereotype is of a lovable nation of charming rogues who can tell you a lie and make you enjoy it. Don't believe the hype, the Italians can be as hard and calculating as anyone, it just suits them to let us think otherwise so they can smile as they drive in the stilletto.

Count Agusta earned his success the hard way, on the racetracks of Europe and he employed heroes like Agostini, Surtees and others to ride his fabulous toys His greatest monument was surely the 500 four; a bike with its soul on fire.

Honda

ome things just look right and the RVF400 is one of them. The whole package simply oozes quality like a 17 jewel movement Rolex. Get in close and check out the details; gold anodized upside down 41mm Showa forks, twin beam aluminium alloy frame, eye-popping Nissin four piston front disc brakes, single sided rear swingarm – need I continue ?

Of course not, because as soon as you see the RVF400 you know that Honda created a banzai bonsai. Like its big brother, the RC45, this is a bespoke bike for the serious scratcher, but in miniature. There's the same Vee shaped, four stroke, four cylinder engine unit at the heart of it, but in the 399cc guise it screams rather than drones. In fact there is no experience in motorcycling so addictive as caning a V4 Honda motor towards a 14,500rpm redline through six gears. Except wearing tasselled leather chaps and a Marlon Brando cap on a Harley, obviously...

But where the RVF400 really comes alive is in the twisties. The ride quality is the very definition of supple, coping with every cack-handed attempt at road repair known to *Daily Star*-reading mankind. It's multi-adjustable at both ends of course, but that sort of fettling only makes a significant difference at a track day, where the RVF400 is capable of utterly humiliating all but the pukka boy racers – regardless of how big their bike, or their bank balance, might be. The way the little Honda turns into a corner so late, even when hard on the brakes until the last tenth of a second, is what sets it apart from the other "grey import" 400 class

VITAL STATISTICS

Engine: 399cc V4 four stroke, water cooled, DOHC, 16 valve, with gear driven camshafts. Gears: six speed. Dry weight: 165kgs. Estimated peak power: 60bhp @ 13,200rpm. Estimated top speed: 125mph.

At just 1395mm, the RVF400's wheelbase is shorter than Mick Doohan's GP bike.

machines. It has real finesse, a dash of handbuilt quality about it that NC30s, GSXR400s etc. all lack. You also need genuine ability to get the very best out of it, so it's a motorcycle for the connoisseur. But unlike exotic Italian race replicas, or the RC45, this is a bike which doesn't cost the earth to own. It can be

had for as little as five grand – the price of a basic retro machine. In that sort of bracket, there's nothing to compare the RVF400 with and the only reason for its existence is that Honda are showing off, again. Great, isn't it ?

> **'there is no experience in motorcycling so addictive as caning a V4 Honda motor towards a 14,500rpm redline through six gears'**

■ **Small, but perfectly formed: the RVF400 was created for the WSB-obsessed home market**

Norton

MANX

The essence of motorcycle

Pure distilled essence of motorcycle. Just look at it. That unburstable big single that came in either 350 or 500cc form and could see out a full season of first class racing and take on the TT without a rebuild. And that double loop cradle frame, the featherbed, which, like all the best ideas in engineering, is the simple solution to all kinds of complex problems. It doesn't matter that if, like me, you were born long after the last Manx rolled out of Norton's works in Bracebridge Street Birmingham, you must surely feel a flush of patriotic pride when you see one. Of course, it could all have been so different.

Norton had debuted a twin-cam single with spectacular success on the Island at the 1927 TT with spectacular results. Norton's development engineer Joe Craig continually developed what was already a very clever design and by the mid-thirties Norton were the team to beat. Which is exactly what an Austrian Alsatian-lover called Adolf Hitler intended to do and didn't care how much it cost. Fortunately, for all of us the Americans won the war (well, they always did in John Wayne films) and after the cessation of hostilities supercharging was banned and BMW had to spend thirty years building bubble cars and clumsy looking tourers for pipe-smoking real ale enthusiasts from Worcester.

It was in 1950 that the legendary status of the Manx was assured when the garden gate was replaced by the featherbed. No, the names weren't the result of someone at Norton having a large piece of shrapnel imbedded in his skull. The 'garden gate' was the old single tube spine frame with 'plunger'

VITAL STATISTICS

349/490cc single cylinder four stroke air cooled engine.
Estimated peak power:
32bhp/48bhp @ 7,000rpm.
Estimated top speed:
105/125mph.
Dry weight: 155/165kgs.
Fuel capacity: 28 litres.

Manx Norton replicas are built somewhere in darkest Wales even today.

suspension and the 'featherbed' was a double-loop cradle frame with a swinging arm and twin shockers suspending the rear wheel, designed by the McCandless brothers, Rex and Cromie.

The featherbed gave the Manx Norton an extension on its racing lifespan, with the added benefit of selling replicas of this legendary bike to the public. No one wants to ride single cylinder bikes now, but the Manx was all that the single could ever be; a century of speed and fluency captured by craftsmen.

❝BMW had to spend thirty years building bubble cars and clumsy looking tourers for pipe-smoking real ale enthusiasts from Worcester❞

■ Geoff Duke, former Grands Prix winning Norton rider in the 1950s, now owns the most successful motorcycle video company in the UK

RD350

Headbanger heaven

 ew Lads ? I fart in their general direction. Every generation thinks its discovered a new way of behaving badly but few can match the anti-social skills displayed by the motley collection of leather clad hooligans aboard their Yamaha RD350LC (LC stood for Liquid Cooled, RD meant Race Developed anorak fans) Castrol R smoking motorcycles.

This was a bike designed to do one thing; kick a great steel toecapped boot in the face of road safety and stamp all over Sir Robert Mark's stringback driving gloves.

It was a two stroke naturally, noisy as a tea chest full of broken china and it emitted a vile cocktail of toxic waste from its exhausts once you opened the throttle beyond 3,000rpm.

But more than that, the 350LC (nicknamed Elsie) was a true streetracer's bike. It had an engine capable of matching sluggardly 750 four strokes up to 90mph, but it also possessed light weight and sharp handling too.

True, early models had front forks made from matchsticks dipped in alloy and barke calipers which seized solid as soon as you spat on them, but the basic ingredients for serious abuse were all there.

Unsurprisingly, it became a dominant choice for the aspiring boy racer, on street or proper racetrack. Yamaha even sponsored the brilliantly chaotic Pro-Am series between 1980-84, which thrilled viewers of World of Sport more used to watching wrestling from Wolverhampton.

■ **Boy toy: the 350LC spawned a cult for lads who knew No Fear**

VITAL STATISTICS

347cc parallel twin, two stroke water cooled engine. Estimated peak power: 58bhp @ 8,500rpm. Estimated top speed: 125mph. Dry weight: 165kgs. Fuel capacity: 18 litres.

Niall Mackenzie was amongst the championship winners inn the Pro-Am series, taking the title in 1984.

> '**a great steel toecapped boot in the face of road safety**'

The second generation LC featured good stuff like the Power Valve, which was a prototype EXUP deal governing exhaust back pressure to boost low end poke, plus a decent fairing and better handling suspension. There was even a relatively comfortable dualseat for brave pillion passengers.

The four strokes caught up eventually and consigned the LC to the dustbin of carbon based life where all two strokes go to die. But in its heyday, it sparked countless incidents of motorcycling insanity on road and track, becoming an archetypal young git's bike, a true, two finger saluting rebel on wheels.

7 Kawasaki

Z1 900

Ultimate 70s muscle bike

When Honda launched their CB750 in 1969 some engineers very nearly fell onto their corporate swords in dismay, for Kawasaki had a secret four cylinder bike project on the go too – Honda had stolen their thunder. But they went back to the drawing board and created what many have described as the definitive 70s Superbike: the Kawasaki Z1 900.

The hot-rod heart of this bike was its double overhead camshaft, 903cc, transverse four cylinder motor. Making 82bhp, it comfortably aced the Honda by over 10bhp and could rocket the rider from standstill to 100mph in a little over 10 seconds. That was the sort of pull which could rip the sideburns off Jason King and crush his velvet loon pants.

But the Kawasaki had an almost indestructible strength in its engine, which made it the power unit choice for drag racing, sidecar madness or 24-hour endurance racers. This motor could take more stick than a Streatham madam on a pound a whack. What's more, it was uncannily smooth and easy to ride. You could tour, ride to work, or play racers all day on a Z1.

Sure, it handled in the Kawasaki tradition, which meant it sort of went like a pinball down a bobsleigh run, and the brakes were so weak that oil tankers could occasionally slip up the inside at roundabouts – but nobody's perfect

The Kawasaki Z1 was proof of the old American adage "There ain't no substitute for cubes", as it earned the respect of other bikers by utterly humiliating them once the road was straight. As it got older, it got bigger and better in the handling and braking departments, but it never lost that big boss reputation throughout the 70s. It also looked badder than James Brown with its stripped down, fastback styling and teardrop fuel tank. In a word, cool.

It was big, it was fast and if you didn't

know how to handle it, things got mean. That was always the essence of the US V8 muscle cars in the 60s and 70s, and the Z1 provided exactly the same kind of speed kick on two wheels.

That's why they called it The King.

'It was big, it was fast, and if you didn't know how to handle it, things got mean'

■ **Fanfare for the Common Man: the King Kwaka brought performance to the people**

6 Aprilia

RS250

Best boy racer 250

Some bikes just look right and this is one of them. A metallic silver 130mph Italian love missile that looks like it's been beamed to Earth from outer space, then sculpted into utter perfection by the ghost of Michelangelo. Do I like it?

No. I absolutely love it.

> **'the Aprilia is every inch the perfect racetrack fantasy machine'**

The real surprise about the Aprilia however is that once you get past the obviously stunning Latin curves, the bike is beautifully impressive to ride. It boasts one of the most completely stable beam-framed alloy chassis in modern biking, married to a Suzuki RGV two stroke Vee twin motor which howls like a banshee above 8,000rpm.

Wherever you point this machine, the rest of it follows about one nanosecond later. As you lean forwards in full Loris Reggiani racing crouch, a digital display just in front of your right eyeball on the dash tells you the water cooled engine temperature, mph and – should you require it – your lap times. Yes, this is boy racer

VITAL STATISTICS

Engine: 90 degree, v-twin, 249cc, liquid cooled, two stroke.
Gears: six speed
Estimated peak power: 60bhp @ 10,500rpm.
Estimated top speed: 130mph.

The Aprilia 250 project developed from racing an Austrian Rotax-engined bike in the late 1980s.

cocaine and you'll find yourself chasing white lines for as long as the sun shines on the road ahead of you.

It has brakes which can stand the bike on its front wheel from 80mph, and it carves high speed corners with eerie stability

Unlike some Japanese 250-class road rockets, the Aprilia is designed to accommodate a human being rather than a ring-tailed lemur, with a decent seat and adequate weather protection from the sexy looking bodywork. It won't beat a moped for commuting, but you can live with it for a day's madcap thrashing about on lazy Sunday afternoons.

From the shark-like tip of its fairing, to the rasping, crackling exhaust noise which sets the hairs on your neck standing up in anticipation, the Aprilia is every inch the perfect racetrack fantasy machine; a virtual reality arcade game come to life.

■ **The sexiest 250 in the world ? Probably**

Honda

Best two-wheeled transport in the history of the world

Honda have sold so many of these that they have virtually stopped counting. It is recognized the world over as the definitive moped, whether it is in 50, 70 or 90cc guise. It can carry entire families in the Third World, work as a mobile shop, tour the globe on about 0.8p per mile, and is so reliable you suspect the engine is like

> **❝the engine is like the car from *Christine* and can rebuild itself should the need arise❞**

what a profound impact it has had on late twentieth century development. No British or Italian scooter could have survived what the C90 has, from Tadcaster to Timbuktu – try riding a Garelli Tiger Cross to Kenya and see how far you get before the engine melts all over your foot.

The Cub supplies that universally

■ **Plastic, but not pony: 20 million-plus buyers, and still selling...**

the car from *Christine* and can rebuild itself should the need arise.

In one barmy moment from the infamous *"Berry On Bikes"* video (available from all good video outlets, very reasonably priced!) we threw a Honda 90 off the edge of a disused quarry to finally destroy it. As we peered over the precipice to witness the shattered wreckage, we could just hear a faint noise: "Phut, phut, phut..."

The thing could only be killed with gelignite detonators. That's tough.

In the 30-odd years since the "Nifty, Thrifty, Honda 50" first appeared in the black and white newspaper adverts, the

world and his wife have phutted to work, or down the shops, on one of these humble commuter machines without realizing

welcome service – basic economic transport. Its plastic bodywork is easily bent straight, and cheap to replace in the event of a crash; its simple four stroke engine is fixable in minutes and does 100mpg no sweat. Furthermore, you can easily junk a wrecked motor from the pressed steel spine frame and slot in another from the scrapyard.

The Cub is simply the Volkswagen Beetle of biking – or the the Model T Ford, the Clarks sandal, the Hoover vacuum cleaner or even the good old Baxi boiler. Every home should have one.

VITAL STATISTICS

Engine: 49cc four stroke, single cylinder, air cooled. Gears: three speed automatic. Estimated peak power: 6.5bhp @ 8,000rpm. Estimated top speed: 35mph.

You can still find fully functional early Honda 50s in auctions from as little as £150.

4

Honda

FIREBLADE CBR900

Best-selling shiny, happy superbike

Just as the GSXR750 changed the way sports bikes looked and behaved in the mid-80s, the Fireblade blew so many minds when it appeared in 1992 that it sent a whole raft of bike designers back to their drawing boards in desperation.

It was lighter, sharper, slicker and plain old faster than the opposition in every way that mattered. For a start, it had an engine which could trickle along smoother than Peter Stringfellow's satin sheets at tick-over,

❛a fantastically accomplished all-round blitzkrieg on two wheels❜

then rocket the rider to 130mph in less time than it takes to say "Is that attractive blonde lady your partner or your daughter?"

The motor was quite simply the benchmark by which other big sportbike power units were judged throughout the decade. It is also reliable to the point of boredom, even if you do have the bottle to regularly cane it – ask Philip McCallen, who has hustled a Fireblade around the Isle of Man TT course

■ **This is the hottest superbike of the 90s**

124

at an average speed of over 120mph. That's an *average* speed, OK?

But the 'Blade wasn't just fast in a straight line, it also handled with the dexterity of a six-fingered card dealer. The chassis was light, yet strong where it counted, and the suspension almost the perfect compromise for outrageous speeds along twisty country roads.

Its closest rival, the Yamaha EXUP 1000, may have had the edge in high speed stability, but the Fireblade could tip into corners and slingshot away a fraction quicker, with the right rider on board, of course. As any racer will tell you, it's that sequence of stuffing a bike in hard on the brakes then getting back on the gas as soon as you can which makes for a truly quick motorcycle.

Soon, the Fireblade became the top selling motorcycle in Britain – even overtaking established volume sellers like the C90 moped. Pretty impressive for a machine which cost about six times as much as a moped. The Fireblade remains a fantastically accomplished all-round blitzkrieg on two wheels today, albeit a little easier to tame. For many bikers, it is quite simply breathtaking.

VITAL STATISTICS

Engine: 918cc DOHC, water cooled, four cylinder, 16 valve, four stroke. Gears: six speed. Estimated peak power: 128bhp @ 10,500rpm. Estimated top speed: 160mph.

A two-grand turbo kit will bring the BHP up to the 175bhp mark at half-boost alone.

ELECTRA GLIDE

All-time classic American motorcycle

Ask one hundred people at random to name any sort of motorcycle and the chances are that over 50 of them would say Harley-Davidson. Furthermore, the image which they carried in their mind would be of the bike you see here – the Electra Glide 1340.

The reasons are simple. The Electra Glide has been part of the scenery in pop videos, movies, fashion magazine shoots, lottery winners' dream garages and a thousand other places in our late twentieth century society. It is an icon of pure Americana, James Dean made metal, a glorious baroque and roll jukebox on wheels. Elvis is probably alive and well and riding an eerie, two-tone, luminous pink Harley somewhere in Nevada right now.

This ornate wedding cake on wheels was born when Harley fitted an electric starter to the land leviathan known as the Duo-

Glide back in the mid-60s. It was a motorcycle designed for those who wanted a bit of comfort whilst they got their kicks on Route 66.

A barndoor-sized windscreen, lazy boy recliner standard seating and luggage-carrying panniers provided the all mod cons for the serious touring rider. Cops rode them too and the image was immortalized in the cult movie *Electra Glide In Blue*.

But like a cathedral built to worship the Great American Dream, any Electra Glide can take a lifetime to completely decorate. The range of accessories for these machines – that's factory options, not the myriad custom supplier kits – is so vast it makes telephone directories look like an easy read.

Leather tassles, art deco tail lights, doe-skin saddles, cruise control throttles, chromosexual spotlights of every conceivable shape and size – the list is almost endless

■ **Electra Glide Orchestra: Harley Davidson have applied to patent the 'potato-potato' beat of their V-twin**

"pure Americana, James Dean made metal, a glorious baroque and roll jukebox on wheels"

extent that only the crankcases remain factory items. The same process can be applied to the braking, electrical and exhaust systems, and, to be honest, they could probably use an upgrade anyway.

The thing is that the Harley-Davidson Electra Glide is something of an anachronism and, to put it crudely, it isn't that brilliant at being ridden at speeds above 65mph. In fact a Gold Wing knocks it into a cocked hat in virtually every area where practical motorcycle engineering counts.

But that's sort of missing the point with the Milwaukee mutha, because the Glide will always be the ultimate iron horse, solid V-twin freedom heading out across the badlands, with the tapedeck playing Springsteen and the engine noise disappearing into the heart of America.

when it comes to making an Electra Glide your own personal statement of two-wheeled freedom. The engine can be tuned, bored and stroked to such a n

VITAL STATISTICS

Engine: 1340cc V-Twin, four stroke, air cooled. Estimated peak power: 60bhp @ 5,000rpm.
Estimated top speed: 105mph.

Yes, Elvis owned one.

127

916

DUCATI

Most erotic exotic bike

The Italians are possibly the most bike crazy nation on Earth; passionate, knowledgeable and completely in love with the art of speed. For them, motorcycles should scream the word speed in big, bold, beautiful, blood red letters. No compromise.

That, in a nutshell, is the philosophy behind designer Tamburini's masterpiece – the 916. Here is sex on wheels. If bikes were a religion, then the Ducati 916 would be the son of God. It really is something unique and bedazzling to look at.

But there's more. Just turn the key and fire up that V-twin engine. The staccato bark as you blip the throttle tells you all you need to

know. This is going to be a total sensory overload, Puccini in motion. This sleek, razor-edged beauty is a perfect marriage of form and function, capa-

■ The Ducati 916 has got to be, quite simply, the best reason for living

ble of blowing your mind standing still or at 150mph. No surprise to anyone with more than a passing interest in engineering, for the 916 is a dedicated to the craft of going fast. A spartan trellis frame holds the motor. The suspension is the best that Japan can mass produce and the brakes are gold coloured Brembos – brick wall stopping power.

Nothing is wasted – there is no excess on this wasp-waisted missile. Everything is designed to contribute to the purpose of going outrageously quickly.

It may be fragile in the transmission and crankcase areas, but every Italian machine has some sort of failing. It's part of the price you pay to own something which wasn't built by committee, by accountants worrying about the cost of the washers. The 916 is human, it's one man's personal vision of motorcycle heaven, a communion with the god of speed, and you have to admire the factory for creating it.

Almost every aspect of the Ducati 916 has influenced biking in the 90s: V-twin engines in sportsbikes, shark-like twin headlights, single coloured bodywork, and the stunning twin exhausts, entwined like a supermodel's legs around the machine. Eat your heart out Michelangelo.

'If bikes were a religion, then the Ducati 916 would be the son of God'

1 R1

Best motorcycle in the world… ever!

This is motorcycling's Golden Age.

Not thirty years ago. Not between the wars. Not when 'British was best' and 'bikes looked like bikes.' Right here, right now. There have never been so many manufacturers utilizing the awesome capabilities of the latest technology – and every last scrap of adventure and imagination in their souls to produce exquistely beautiful and fantastically capable bikes. And the best bit is that it doesn't matter what you ride – whether you're into dual purpose offroaders, chrome-laden factory customs, stroker scratchers or continent crushing grand tourers – there is an embarrassment of brilliant bikes vying for your hard-earned cash. If you're looking for the most exciting and adictive adrenalin rush available in non-powdered form then you need look no further. All of this has been leading up to something – and it's something that when I started out to write this book I never imagined I would find myself saying – the best bike in the world isn't a Ducati.

The R1 is built in a factory in Japan, probaby by machines – and d'you know what? I couldn't care less.

The R1 really is that good. I always knew Yamaha had it in them, yet. it was still a shock of seismic proptions when they published the figures. The R1 accelerates stronger, stops surer, turns quicker into a corner, drives harder and faster out of it than any other road bike you have ever ridden. And I mean you, not some hot-headed roadtester with a desk drawer full of speeding tickets and a garage full of other people's broken bikes. And that's the real beauty of it, because the R1 doesn't hide its performance away in the faraway reaches of the rev range where it can only be found by riders born and bred on a racetrack. It's right there from 3,000rpm to the 12,000rpm redline and you can have as much or as little of it as you like.

Yamaha went to war on weight when they built the R1. It was lost by all manner of engineering alchemy too intricate to relate here but if you get off on that sort of thing then I suggest you keep the handbook in locked drawer so you can slaver over it in private. Wear loose-fitting tousers. By casting the cylinder block and crankcase in one piece they allowed much of the chassis to be jettisoned and the engine itself to be used as a stressed member.

Stressed members also come to mind when you look at the thing. Until the R1 was unleashed I believed the best looking Japanese bike of all time was the ill-fated Suzuki TL1000, although obviously that was because it was so much a 916 wannabe. The Yamaha R1 doesn't need to steal anyone elses clothes even if they do carry the most exclusive Italian designer label. Quite simply it is the best looking bike ever built outside of Italy.

So for all sorts of reasons the Yamaha R1 is my choice for the best bike of all time but don't just take my word for it – get out there and grab every opportunity to ride as many bikes as you can (yes, crap ones as well – it'll give you perspective) and you could have a whole lot of fun proving that I'm wrong.

quite simply, it is the best looking bike ever built outside of Italy

■ A stunning synthesis of everything that makes modern motorcycles pure adrenalin on wheels

THE DOGS
OF THE ROAD

ex.
Motorcycling and sex have enjoyed an energetic and mutually satisfying relationship ever since Sigmund Freud's secretary suggested that she'd like to feel something powerful throbbing between her legs and Sigmund turned up at the clinic the next day on his well-fitted big single.

Of course there are certain people who insultingly infer that those of us who ride unfeasibly large motorcycles are compensating for the fact that we're hung like hamsters. Utter nonsense but, just for the record, can I say that I'm the proud owner of a Puch Pansy 50cc Scooterette.

No, the single thing that couples motorcycling and sex tighter than a pair of council estate strays in a heatwave is that when they're good they're very, very good and when they're bad they're still pretty damn fine.

Except for this lot. If they were blokes instead of bikes they'd still live at home with their mothers and have an unnatural interest in Airfix kits and Jill Dando.

And rather than fill this section with the downtrodden donkeys that occasionally escape from the old communist bloc, I've decided to concentrate instead on shaming those who really ought to have known better.

Yes, if motorcyling can be compared to sex, then riding any of these is like kissing your granny at Christmas and finding out that she 'does tongues'...

MOTO 6.5

Art with a capital F

ow hard can it be to make a motorcycle look good? Well, you wouldn't think it was rocket science, would you? Nevertheless, the evidence of history provides a telling indictment of aesthetic aberrations and bastard-ugly bikes.

Rumour has it that while the Moto 6.5 was being made at the Noale factory, workers had to be told they were producing targets for the Italian army and that the peculiar circular shape would show up better on radar. When they learned the awful truth many were seen weeping openly at the factory gates. The bloke responsible was madcap lemon-squeezer stylist Phillippe Starck. He is French, but then you already guessed that. His philosophy was to re-invent the motorcycle so that it would appeal to non-bikers. And the thing about the motorcycle is that it doesn't need re-inventing, we like it the way it is.

At five grand a go they probably shifted a few to advertising executives, satellite TV

> **'the perpetrators of this crime have no excuse'**

presenters and the sort of speccy toffs who turn up on Channel Four going on about 'grasping the zeitgeist'. I know what I'd like to grasp. How did it ride? Well, I was the first person outside the factory to do so (yeah, BIG THRILL) and to be honest the five-valve Austrian Rotax was willing enough but the handling was all to cock because the pretentious Parisian insisted on old-style rubber because new stuff 'wasn't fashionable enough.' Is it any wonder so many people have declared war on the French? The Aprilia Moto 6.5 – a bold

style statement for rich urban bikers destined to be matt-blacked and despatched to death in a big city near you. Soon.

■ **Stark Style: one of his 'designer' toothbrushes will set you back forty quid**

Honda

NR500

The 'Nearly Ready' Racer

In 1979 Honda's corporate hospitality machine steamrollered the tiny minds of British road racing journalists with two pieces of shock news; firstly, they were returning to Grands Prix racing after a decade long absence and secondly, they were competing on a 500cc four stroke, V4 shaped, oval pistoned, monocoque chassis motorcycle which revved to an astounding 22,000rpm.

Were they mad?

Yes, as it turned out. Totally barking.

The new four stroke racer was in fact a V8 engined bike, with the neat trick of oval pistons, dual conrods and twin spark plugs effectively halving the number of combustion chambers to comply with the FIM rules. Honda had obviously been quietly fuming since anything with more than four cylinders was banned from GP racing and seemed determined to prove – at a cost of millions – that four strokes could compete with Suzuki and Yamaha two strokes.

Interestingly the man in charge of the project was called Mr. Fukui – which may have been an example of Japanese humour, but we'll never know for sure.

The NR500's debut at Silverstone a month later was slightly embarrassing. Mutton-chopped Yorkshire superstar, Mick Grant fell off at the first corner and the bike exploded into a ball of flame. Japanese ace Katayama managed to survive five laps before his bike expired – he was running second to last at the time.

Honda went away to sulk in a corner and dream up more ways of spending a few million yen on dinky toy 16-inch wheels and fettling the ill-handling one piece section aluminium chassis. The French GP at the end of season saw the NR500 return, like Lazarus from the dead.

Sadly, both bikes were so slow that they failed to qualify for any of the 40 grid places in the 500cc GP race. Oh Fukui...

The writing was on the wall, Honda had blown it. They 'suspended' the NR project at the start of 1982. Yet to the bitter end, they refused to admit it had been a colossal waste of time and money. Honda maintained that 'valuable lessons and new technologies were learned' from the NR500 fiasco.

Yeah, maybe so in terms of piston ring trickery, multi-valve cylinder head gasflowing and so on. But after competing well in a few endurance races in the late '80s, the result of all this expertise, the NR750 flagship roadbike weighed 100lbs more than a Yamaha EXUP, was at least 15mph slower, yet cost £32,000 to buy. Insane.

> **he fell at the first corner and the bike burst into a ball of flame**

■ Sad to say, but this bike provides the best reason to fall on your ceremonial sword

GTS1000

Yamaha

Biggest Corporate White Elephant of the 90s

■ **Yamaha sold about 15 of these overweight behemoths in the UK**

and doesn't scare the rest of the cul-de-sac. See the catalytic coverter and, if you wanted it, the reassurance of ABS braking. Loads of weight and a low centre of gravity promised a smooth and relaxing ride but made the steering slovenly. Sound familiar? That's right – its a bloody car. A big fat nylon underpants-wearing, antiques-roadshow-watching, two-wheeled car to take you to the garden centre every Sunday... for the rest of your life.

Motorcycles like the Yamaha GTS1000 are simply not worthy of the name because they deny the danger and excise the excitement. They want to steal the soul of motorcycling for their own sick purpose. They want to create... the Anti-bike.

They should be hunted down and put out of their misery like the rabid mongrels they are.

> **'They want to steal the soul of motorcycling for their own sick purpose'**

What young man with red blood coursing through his veins, angry zits on his face and a dangerous fixation (bordering on stalking) for the captain of he sixth form netball team hasn't been seduced by the pant-stiffening appeal of motorcycling? The attraction is easy enough to explain – where else are you going to get the heady combination of personal freedom allied to affordabilty and of course all served up with a powerful whiff of danger? Who could resist? Well, not me for a start and probably not you either. However, there are those among us who have made it their task to produce

a powered two-wheeler with none of the fuel to fire adolescent imaginations and not one pant of the passion that produces a life long love of biking.

What is worse is that it should be Yamaha who should be exposed in such an insidious and reprellant endeavour. Surely they could be trusted to do the right thing? From LC to FZR to R1 they've given us so much. So when the hub-centered steered GTS1000 surfaced in 1994 looking, sounding and behaving every bit like a two-wheeled company Cavalier it was like finding out that Rolf Harris takes his holidays in Korea because he likes the taste of dog.

Just look at it if you can without the bile in your stomach rising in protest. See the sensible paint scheme that hides the dirt

VITAL STATISTICS

**Engine: 1002cc four cylinder four stroke water cooled engine.
Estimated peak power: 100bhp @ 9,500rpm.
Estimated top speed: 135mph.
Dry weight: 265kgs.
Fuel capacity: 21 litres.**

Honda tried racing a GP bike with hub centre steering for most of the 80s. Despite the power of Ron Haslam's sideburns, it failed to win.

Fantic

CHOPPER 125

Best argument against legalizing drugs

o I really need to say anything? The answer is, of course, no, but the opportunity is just too good to miss. I want you to do something for me, I want you to tear this page from its binding and stick it in your wallet. The next time anyone starts telling you the Italians are the most stylish nation alive pull it out and demand an explanation.

Fantic are, of course, the motorcycle manufacturer most likely to be represented among the fire engines, space rockets and flying elephants in the kiddies korner at the fun fair. The Fantic Chopper was, of course, inspired by Peter Fonda's Panhead Harley Captain America, at once a link with the cowboys of the Wild West and the free-wheeling freaks of the San Francisco scene. Riding a hard-tailed hog was part of an unwritten language and signalled to other open-minded people that you were a fully subscribed contributor to the counterculture. However, riding a Fantic chopper also said something about you: it said you were a twat. Rather than surfing the never-ending wave of full-fat torque from a titanic v-twin, Fantic riders found their progress accompanied by the shriek of a single cylinder 125cc two stroke. Harley riders only change gear when a new president is elected but Fantic riders had to shift cogs like their life depended on it if they wanted to outrun nuns in Fiat 500s.

The cycle parts though were absolutely authentic – long extended forks, high ape-hanger handlebars and a backrest so ludicrously large it could be doubled-up as an ironing board for crease-conscious style warriors. Surprisingly, most reports said the handling and brakes weren't that bad – but, as you'd have to wire the contents of my Calvins to the mains before I'd agree to swing a leg across this cockeyed cack-handed custom, I suppose I'll never know.

Now, the Raleigh Chopper, there were some kick-ass wheels.

> ❝Harley riders only change gear when a new president is elected❞

■ **Fantically my dear, I don't give a damn: it even looked crap in the 70s**

136

TIGER CROSS

Best candidate for fairground roundabout

■ **Easy, Tiger: even a free t-shirt wouldn't persuade you to buy one**

suited to a Massey Ferguson than a moped and brakes from a bicycle repair shop. It was also usually coloured a rancid shade of red or yellow to add further pain to anyone who saw, or heard it razz along their street. Normally though, a Tiger Cross wouldn't even start in the first place, so dicing with AP50s or FS1Es wasn't on the cards.

Truly revolting in every way, the Garelli's only use in society was to keep bored skinheads off the highways and broken down on some farm track, as they attempted to try some off-road moped mayhem at weekends, whilst ripped out of their tiny minds on Woodpecker cider.

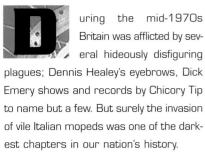

uring the mid-1970s Britain was afflicted by several hideously disfiguring plagues; Dennis Healey's eyebrows, Dick Emery shows and records by Chicory Tip to name but a few. But surely the invasion of vile Italian mopeds was one of the darkest chapters in our nation's history.

Suddenly, a large minority of the country's flare clad teenagers were convinced that products bearing the name Minarelli, Fantic, Malagutti or Italjet were likely to transport them to that job as an apprentice in the Chrysler Avenger factory on time. Worst of all perhaps, amongst a gabble of smoking, screeching, unreliable shite, was the Garelli Tiger Cross – although the Rekord was pretty foul too.

The Tiger Cross was an early attempt at convincing the gullible 16-year-olds that they were getting more for their parents'

> **❝it was an early attempt at convincing 16-year-olds that they were getting more for their money by making the bike look bigger than it was❞**

money by making the bike look bigger than it was. The Cross boasted a tubular steel cradle frame, which stood proud and tall in the enduro style, with farty 6 volt lighting and big mudguards attached to it.

The engine unit was 49cc of pure petroil drinking poison, which would seize up if you so much as urinated in its general direction. With an odd-looking radial finned cylinder head, it spluttered and gasped for air through its leaking carburettor like a rutting bison wearing a gas mask.

Other problems included a seat which was held on with what appeared to be an old woman's hairgrip, an air filter more

VITAL STATISTICS

Engine: 49cc single cylinder, two stroke, air cooled engine. **Lubrication;** oil mixed with petrol. **Gears:** four speed – later models had a five speed option. **Estimated peak power:** 6bhp @ 8,000rpm. **Estimated top speed** 40mph. **Dry weight:** 163lbs.

Garellis were imported by Agrati in Nottingham, who also brought in all Kawasaki motorcycles until 1976.

Suzuki

RE5 ROTARY

Worst rotary nightmare

The world is littered with the broken, empty dreams of madcap engineers, chancers and the clinically insane. Such a mind undoubtedly brought forth the rotary engine – a petrol powered dishwasher pump for cars and bikes. In fact, it was a German called Dr Felix Wankel, which should have alerted someone at Suzuki...

The RE5 was a huge disaster of almost Titanic proportions. Suzuki invested over two million pounds in setting up a pro-

> **❝What was wrong with the RE5? Everything❞**

duction line dedicated to churning out this overweight, spluttering, gas guzzling monstrosity, topped off by its infamous "Swiss roll" dashboard display.

Even in 1972 that was pure folly, and when the RE5 hit the streets the following year – just as the Arab world demanded six times more dollars per barrel for their crude oil – Suzuki realized it had dropped a bollock so big that NASA thought they'd discovered a new planet.

What was wrong with the RE5? Everything. Its complex engine had problems with overheating rotor tips. The carburettor – which needed five cables to operate – never delivered the same fuel charge twice. It was very, very heavy, the brakes didn't work when it rained and the double skinned exhausts rusted from the inside. Need anything more?

OK then: it drank petrol at about 30mpg on a good day, the chrome plating peeled like a ginger-haired man on holiday in the Gobi desert and it handled worse than a drunken hippo on rollerblades. Its standard tyres also appeared to be made of old Bakelite wireless sets.

A desperate update in 1974 failed to convince the world that the Suzuki corporate flagship was the cutting edge of 70s Superbiking and the whole project was placed in the drawer marked "Living Nightmares" back at the factory. A classic example of deranged engineers trying to foist their ideas of what bikes should be about onto an uninterested public. The only good rotary is a clothes dryer in the back garden.

■ 'Wanklers' is the correct term for enthusiasts of Dr Felix's rotary engine

XLCR CAFE RACER

Worst Harley ever made **1000**

Stick to what you know. It's sound advice, which is nevertheless routinely ignored by soccer players every time someone utters the phrase, "Let's do a pop record lads!"

Several people at Harley-Davidson back in the 70s should have also listened to that old saying before assisting in the birth of one sad, sick and sorry-looking excuse for a motorbike. The XLCR 1000 was surely one of the most horrible, deeply unpleasant ways of wasting thousands of pounds known to man this side of paying to watch *Riverdance*.

The tragedy of it all was of course that a Harley cafe racer could have been so mean, so moody, so dark chocolate sex on wheels.

However, back in grim reality, what we're looking at is basically a tarted up 1950s Sportster with the XR750 flat tracker bike's rear end slapped on.

'one of the most horrible, deeply unpleasant ways of wasting thousands of pounds known to man'

■ **Sad Café: It looked great, it sounded great, but it went like an invalid carriage towing a caravan**

The "sporty" one litre engine was affectionately known as one an ironhead – but by the 70s, these motors had got further past their sell-by date than a meat pie in a lay-by snack van. It shook, it cracked the frame, and it got very hot and bothered, especially if you did something rash like open the throttle too far beyond 70mph.

In return for all this sound and fury, all the hapless owner got was a claimed 68bhp, rattled out at around 6,000rpm. The truth was much more mundane, with something in the order of 50bhp on tap if you were lucky, although repeated attempts to make the XLCR go quickly would be met with extreme prejudice by the engine internals.

In plain English, the dog would puke its guts over your boots, boy.

Things were no better in the handling department, where a Triumph Bonneville could simply disappear into the distance whilst the Harley struggled to keep the road. With the ground clearance of a knock-kneed newt and the weight of a pregnant hippo, the Harley was a regular menace to society.

On top of this nightmare concoction, the rider sat perched like a dead parrot nailed to a plank, soaking up huge waves of brain-crumbling vibration, and wondering what the hell he was going to collide with when the brakes finally decided to give up and disintegrate. Oh, did I forget to mention the truly appalling disc brakes, which were apparently made from old records?

Sorry, the brakes were crap too.

So, to recap, we have an engine with feeble, useless power attached to a weedy frame, rock-hard suspension, duff brakes and tyres made of Bakelite. The only two-wheeled thing that this bike could conceivably race to a cafe would be a Reliant Robin with one wheel stolen…

Yet in its all-black, satin crackled paintwork, and lean and hungry lines, the XLCR was close to a good looking motorcycle. It had American brutality oozing from every iron lump and crudely curvaceous panel. It could've been a contender.

As it was, every last XLCR should have been buried under a bridge in New Jersey like an anonymous victim of the mob, never to insult any motorcyclist again by firing its wheezing turnip thresher of an engine.

Please, don't ever make me think about it again.

VITAL STATISTICS

Engine: 997cc 45 degree V-twin four stroke, air cooled. Gears: four speed. Estimated peak power: 50bhp @ 6,000rpm. Estimated top speed: 105mph.

Although the XLCR ran with a dry sump engine, it needed an astonishing seven and a half pints of oil pumping around to keep from seizing solid.

Kawasaki

Z1R TURBO

Quickest route to casualty

Don't get me wrong I like Americans. I also like dogs and children. It's just that I just wouldn't want to trust any of them with the keys for something large and potentially life-threatening like a combine harvester, a nuclear submarine, or, God forbid, a motorcycle. Essentially the strumbling block towards effective operation is the same for each of the three groups – the problem is believing you can never have too much of a good thing: Pedigree Chum, talking Teletubbies or mountains of horsepower – it doesn't make any difference.

This doesn't apply to Americans, however. How else do you explain a car like the Dodge Coronet? A three-box behemoth weighing in at around two tons manufactured by the Chrysler Corporation and offered to the good people of the United States with crossply rubber tyres,

drum brakes and, get this, a 426 horse-power V8 engine. In the mid 60s such satanic sedans accounted for more fatalities among young American males then the concerted efforts of the Viet Cong.

Therefore it should come as no surprise that the Americans were entirely responsible for the Kawasaki Z1R Turbo – an ill-advised attempt to squeeze more performance from a motorcycle that was never really up to the job of handling it – but a damn fine way of finding out once and for all if there is life after death.

Kaswasaki supplied brand new Z1Rs to the American distributor who gave them a fab and groovy paintjob and nailed on a turbo charger usually found helping small jet aircraft stay on course over Central America. Kawasaki disowned them and wouldn't work on them or allow them to be exported anywhere as a very

sensible corporate safety policy.

The sad truth of it all was that the stock Z1R was already borderline homicidal in terms of handling and duff brakes, without bolting another 30bhp onto its engine. Mad and very, very bad.

VITAL STATISTICS

Engine: 1015cc four cylinder transverse four stroke air cooled engine. Estimated peak power: 125bhp @ 9,000rpm. Estimated top speed: 145mph. Dry weight: 205kgs. Fuel capacity: 17 litres.

Z1R brakes suffered from 'wet weather lag' which meant you had to wait a second for them to start working in the rain. Nice.

> **‟a damn fine way of finding out once and for all if there is life after death”**

■ Ooh ah Z1R; a bike as bad as the Daily Star... edited by Americans

1000

The Great British Cock-Up

Hesketh

Do you remember *Ripping Yarns*? 'Across The Andes By Frog', 'Barnstoneworth–bloody–united'? 'Hesketh' would have made a great Ripping Yarn: a well-bred British world beater built with plenty of pluck and spunk sees off Johnny Foreigner and his horrible cheap gaudy motorbikes. Hurrah for his Lordship and his large capacity V-twin grand touring motorcycle! The only trouble was that 'Hesketh' wasn't a half-hour comedy drama – although there was a good degree of both comedy and drama involved – but an ill-fated attempt to revive the rotting corpse of the British bike industry.

The Japanese usually get the blame for undermining our glorious tradition of motorcycle manufacture but the truth is that we could probably have managed just as well without them. Underdevelopment and a lack of investment meant that many manufacturers were still offering their post-war product, with one or two alterations, in the sixties. When they realised that they were about to go bust many sought salvation in mopeds and scooters and produced some quite astonishingly inept and ugly machines. Lord Alexander Hesketh wanted to build a gentleman's sporting motorcycle in the grand tradition of JAP Brough Superior and of HRD Vincent. He failed. Choice components were gathered from around the globe: Astralite wheels, Marzochoci suspension, Weaslake engine. That's right – the speedway people.

The Hesketh V1000 first appeared in 1980 and some members of the journalistic community, no doubt dazzled by the affable aristocrat's legendary hospitality, wrote chest-beating, flag-waving nonsense about the rebirth of the great British bike. Well if it was a rebirth then it was

VITAL STATISTICS

Engine: 1000cc four stroke, liquid cooled 90 degree V–Twin.
Estimated peak power: 82hp @ 6,000 rpm.
Estimated top speed: 120mph.

Until recently the original V1000 and a wild–looking variant called the Vortan were being built to order. Priced at £8,000 and £20,000 respectively. Fancy one? No. And neither did anyone else.

a difficult pregnancy followed by an emergency caesarean. If it had been a dog or horse they would have taken it out and shot it, if it had been a child they would have locked it in an attic room and forbade the servants to ever acknowledge its existence. But, because it was a bike, they spent two years trying to sort out its problems before putting it on sale in 1982. And – guess what? They failed. The gearbox was terrible and the hugely heavy 90 degree V–twin sounded like... well a couple of speedway bikes. It was porous and it leaked oil. And

■ **Oh My Lord; 'Bubbles' Hesketh loved his aristocratic folly. Bikers hated it**

anyhow the weird beards who derive sordid pleasure from the crude habits of overweight and underdeveloped European tackle, like the Hesketh , were already well catered for by the range of agricultural implements offered by both BMW and Moto Guzzi. The company went bust, having built less than 150 bikes.

You should never treat the past with too much respect. A belief that British is always best by some sort of hereditary right will only ever lead you one place: the dole office.

❛I don't think his lordship ended up selling *The Big Issue*❜

Velocette

VICEROY

Worst excuse for a scooter ever

The Viceroy sums up everything you need to know about the casually inept thinking which the British motorcycle industry managed in response to the scooter boom of the 1950s.

Suddenly, cheap credit and the end of rationing provoked a transport boom and the Italian scooters from Vespa and Lambretta appealed the new, beatnik generation. For some strange reason, the best that Triumph, BSA and many other factories could come up with was to lash their foulest proprietary bought-in engines to their worst selling lightweight machines, then stick some tin plate around the entire mess. Triumph did it with their Tina and Tigress 250 scooters, Sun compounded errors by fitting 15 inch wheels onto their Geni 100 model too – basically, all the Brits were trying to disguise the fact that it was an enclosed motorbike. They were too ashamed to admit that they really didn't have a clue.

The Viceroy however, was truly awe-

some in its awfulness, being the twisted offspring from another failed concept, the Velocette LE. This had a 200cc two stroke flat twin engine attached to a pressed steel frame and was supposed to be a real groundbreaking design, like the Ariel Leader. It did cause some ground-breaking in the early 60s, as people prepared a hole in which they buried the hideously slow, unreliable Vogue and waited for the entire Velocette factory to follow its product into history.

With innovative features like shaft drive optional twin headlights, panniers etc. the Vogue was a good pocket sized touring bike, but there were two big problems in that department; first, no one wanted a

small touring bike and secondly, if they did, the Vogue would'be broken down in your driveway whilst you fastened the straps on your waxproofed jodphurs.

The whole point about scooters – fixing the engine next to the driven rear wheel on a monococque chassis – was entirely missed by Velocette and all the other British manufacturers. Their feeble, Heath-Robinson approach probably did more to push people into cars than all the Mod vs Rocker hype ever did in the 60s. Thank Christ the Japanese came along and put these pipe smoking buffoons out of their misery.

> 'The Viceroy was truly awesome in its awfulness, being the twisted offspring from another failed concept, the Velocette LE'

■ **The English vice; only masochists could enjoy riding such half-baked nonsense.**

VITAL STATISTICS

Engine: 249cc flat twin, four stroke air cooled engine.
Estimated peak power: 12bhp @ 5,500rpm.
Estimated top speed: 55mph.
Dry weight: 165kgs.
Fuel capacity: 18 litres.

Although dealers flogged over 100,000 scooters in 1959, by 1964, sales had dropped almost 70% – that's when the Viceroy was launched.

INDEX

PICTURE CREDITS

The publishers would like to thank
the following sources for their kind
permission to reproduce the pictures
in this book:

Aprilia Moto (UK) Ltd: 108, 109.
Moto Cinelli International Ltd: 61,
  84.
BMW (GB) Ltd: 50, 73.
Jeff Hackett: 85
Honda (U.K.): 13, 30, 38, 80, 89, 95
Kawasaki: 12, 14, 25, 36, 74
**Don Morley International Sports
  Photo Agency**: 8, 9, 11, 12, 15,
  16, 17, 18, 19, 22, 24, 26, 28,
  29, 40, 41, 45, 47, 51, 54, 55,
  56, 57, 58, 59, 62, 63, 64 tr, 69,
  71, 72, 75, 86, 90, 91, 93, 94,
  103, 110, 111, 112, 113, 114,
  115, 116, 117, 118, 119, 123,
  124, 125, 134, 138, 139, 142
Andrew Morland: 6, 20, 32, 46, 64,
  66, 68, 78, 79, 102, 121, 141
The National Motor Museum: 34, 44,
  87, 92

Kenny P: 140
Quadrant Picture Library: 10, 35,
  42, 88, 135, Roland Brown 31,
  140; Simon Everett 33; Gold &
  Goose 122; Phil Masters 80
Sports Moped Owners Club: 67.
  Triumph Motorcycles Ltd: 77.
  Matthew Ward: 2, 3, 4, 48, 49,
  52, 53, 100, 101, 102, 104, 105,
  106, 128, 129
**The World's Motorcycles News
  Agency**: 21, 23, 27, 37, 39, 130,
  131. 81, 98, 99, 133, 136, 137.
  Yamaha Motor (UK) Ltd: 43.

Every effort has been made to
acknowledge correctly and contact
the source and/or copyright holder of
each picture, and Carlton Books Limited
apologises for any unintentional errors
or omissions which will be corrected in
future editions of this book.